LIVING IN
THE GRIP OF
RELENTLESS
GRACE

THE GOSPEL ACCORDING TO
THE OLD TESTAMENT

A series of studies on the lives
of Old Testament characters, written for
laypeople and pastors, and designed to
encourage Christ-centered reading, teaching,
and preaching of the Old Testament.

TREMPER LONGMAN III
J. ALAN GROVES

Series Editors

After God's Own Heart, by Mark J. Boda
Crying Out for Vindication, by David R. Jackson
Faith in the Face of Apostasy, by Raymond B. Dillard
From Famine to Fullness, by Dean R. Ulrich
Hope in the Midst of a Hostile World, by George M.
  Schwab
Immanuel In Our Place, by Tremper Longman III
Living in the Gap Between Promise and Reality, by
  Iain M. Duguid
Living in the Grip of Relentless Grace, by Iain M. Duguid
Love Divine and Unfailing, by Michael P. V. Barrett
Salvation Through Judgment and Mercy, by
  Bryan D. Estelle
Longing for God in an Age of Discouragement, by
  Bryan Gregory
Right in Their Own Eyes, by George M. Schwab

LIVING IN

THE GRIP OF

RELENTLESS

GRACE

THE GOSPEL IN THE LIVES OF
ISAAC & JACOB

IAIN M. DUGUID

P&R
PUBLISHING
P.O. BOX 817 • PHILLIPSBURG • NEW JERSEY 08865-0817

Unless otherwise indicated, all Scripture quotations are from the HOLY BIBLE, NEW INTERNATIONAL VERSION®. NIV®. Copyright © 1973, 1978, 1984 by International Bible Society. Used by permission of Zondervan Publishing House. All rights reserved.

Other Scripture quotations are from the New American Standard Bible. Copyright by the Lockman Foundation 1960, 1962, 1963, 1968, 1971, 1973, 1975, 1977.

Printed in the United States of America

Library of Congress Cataloging-in-Publication Data

Duguid, Iain M.
     Living in the grip of relentless grace : the Gospel in the lives of Isaac and Jacob / Iain M. Duguid.
          p.   cm.—(The Gospel according to the Old Testament)
     Includes bibliographical references and index.
     ISBN-10: 0-87552-655-1 (pbk.)
     ISBN-13: 978-0-87552-655-3 (pbk.)
     1. Isaac (Biblical patriarch) 2. Jacob (Biblical patriarch)
3. Bible. O.T. Genesis XXV, 19–XXXV, 29—Criticism, interpreta-tion, etc. 4. Bible. O.T. Genesis—Relation to the New Testament. 5. Bible. N.T.—Relation to the Old Testament. I. Title. II. Series.

BS580.I67 D84 2002
222'.1106—dc21
                                                            2002028539

CONTENTS

FOREWORD

The New Testament is in the Old concealed;
the Old Testament is in the New revealed.
    —Augustine

Concerning this salvation, the prophets, who spoke of the grace that was to come to you, searched intently and with the greatest care, trying to find out the time and circumstances to which the Spirit of Christ in them was pointing when he predicted the sufferings of Christ and the glories that would follow. It was revealed to them that they were not serving themselves but you, when they spoke of the things that have now been told you by those who have preached the gospel to you by the Holy Spirit sent from heaven. Even angels long to look into these things. (1 Peter 1:10–12)

"In addition, some of our women amazed us. They went to the tomb early this morning but didn't find his body. They came and told us that they had seen a vision of angels, who said he was alive. Then some of our companions went to the tomb and found it just as the women had said, but him they did not see." He said to them, "How foolish you are, and how slow of heart to believe all that the prophets have spoken! Did not the Christ have to suffer these things and then enter his glory?" And beginning with Moses and all the Prophets, he explained to them what was said in all the Scriptures concerning himself. (Luke 24:22–27)

The prophets searched. Angels longed to see. And the disciples didn't understand. But Moses, the prophets, and all the Old Testament Scriptures had spoken about it— that Jesus would come, suffer, and then be glorified. God began to tell a story in the Old Testament, the ending for which the audience eagerly anticipated. But the Old Testament audience was left hanging. The plot was laid out, but the climax was delayed. The unfinished story begged an ending. In Christ, God has provided the climax to the Old Testament story. Jesus did not arrive unannounced; his coming was declared in advance in the Old Testament, not just in explicit prophecies of the Messiah but by means of the stories of all of the events, characters, and circumstances in the Old Testament. God was telling a larger, overarching, unified story. From the account of creation in Genesis to the final stories of the return from exile, God progressively unfolded his plan of salvation. And the Old Testament account of that plan always pointed in some way to Christ.

AIMS OF THIS SERIES

The Gospel According to the Old Testament Series is committed to the proposition that the Bible, both Old and New Testaments, is a unified revelation of God and that its thematic unity is found in Christ. The individual books of the Old Testament exhibit diverse genres, styles, and individual theologies, but tying them all together is the constant foreshadowing of, and pointing forward to, Christ. Believing in the fundamentally Christocentric nature of the Old Testament, as well as the New Testament, we offer this series of studies in the Old Testament with the following aims:

- to lay out the pervasiveness of the revelation of Christ in the Old Testament
- to promote a Christ-centered reading of the Old Testament
- to encourage Christ-centered preaching and teaching from the Old Testament

To this end, the volumes in this series are written for pastors and laypeople, not scholars.

While such a series could take a number of different shapes, we have decided, in most cases, to focus individual volumes on Old Testament figures—people—rather than books or themes. Some books, of course, will receive major attention in connection with their authors or main characters (e.g., Daniel or Isaiah). Also, themes will be emphasized in connection with particular figures.

It is our hope and prayer that this series will revive interest in and study of the Old Testament as readers recognize that the Old Testament points forward to Jesus Christ.

TREMPER LONGMAN III
J. ALAN GROVES

ACKNOWLEDGMENTS

Almost every time I stand to preach in front of God's people, I pray the same simple prayer: "Lord, these are your sheep and this is your Word. Please feed your sheep from your Word and may you be glorified." The material in these chapters originated as sermons delivered to Redeemer Presbyterian Church in Oxford, England, which were then reworked and developed for Grace Presbyterian Church (PCA) in Fallbrook, California. The two congregations were very different geographically and demographically, but are linked by a common love for God and his grace and a delight in his Word. God's Word remains good food for his sheep the world over. It is my prayer that you too will be fed from this solid food and that God will receive all the glory.

Many people have contributed to the making of this book. Al Groves and Tremper Longman were my teachers in seminary and now, as series editors, they continue to clarify my thinking with useful comments and advice. Linda Triemstra and Thom Notaro also carefully read and corrected the manuscript. My wife, Barb, is always my most discerning critic and best friend, constantly pointing me back to the gospel and challenging me to apply it to my own heart and life. My children, Jamie, Sam, Hannah, Robbie, and Rosie, are the best front row audience any preacher could wish for.

Part of the revision of the manuscript was done while in Scotland for a last visit with my mother, Eileen Duguid, who has now gone to be in God's closer presence. She encouraged and nurtured my earliest interest in God's Word and actively distributed her little boy's books to anyone who could be persuaded to read them. This book is therefore affectionately dedicated to her memory.

INTRODUCTION:

RELENTLESS GRACE

With the death of Abraham and his burial in the Promised Land (Gen. 25:7–11), his part in the story of redemption came to an end. Abraham fought the good fight, persevered to the end, and the torch passed on to his descendants. In the last part of Genesis 25, therefore, we move into a new era, marked by the formula "This is the account of Abraham's son Isaac" (Gen. 25:19). Here the story begins of Isaac and Rebekah and of their sons Jacob and Esau. This is the story of the next generations, those who are assigned the task of following in the shadow of greatness. How will they measure up to the spiritual legacy they have inherited from their father?

The Bible is not particularly flattering to those whose lives it records: the account is faithful, warts and all. In my earlier book, *The Gospel According to Abraham*, we saw that there were quite a few ups and downs in the life of Abraham, the great man of faith. But at least Abraham had some ups. The few events recorded of Isaac's life are mostly downs, and Jacob is no great hero, especially in his early life. They do not begin to live up to the pattern set for them.

There should be great encouragement here for those of us who are all too aware of our shortcomings. Has God called you to perform tasks for which you feel totally inadequate? Cheer up! You are almost certainly right in your assessment. In yourself, you very likely do not have the power to do what God is asking you to do. I become daily more aware of my assorted weaknesses, failings, and sins, and I marvel that God could nonetheless use someone like me in ministry. But our God delights in writing straight with a crooked pencil. He delights in using clay pots in which to store his treasure. The reason for this is simple. His strength is most abundantly seen in our weakness, and his glory most apparent when he uses the most insignificant people to bring about his wonderful purposes (2 Cor. 4:7).

In the lives of Isaac and Jacob, this principle is abundantly clear. We will see time and time again how God in his grace and for his glory overrules the weakness and sinfulness of his chosen instruments. Step by step, God was continuing to fulfill his promise to Abraham to turn a small family into a mighty nation (Gen. 15:5). There is substantial progress toward the goal of God's plan in these pages. But from the outset, it is to be made clear to Israel—as it should also be clear to us—that the gospel triumphs not through might or through human goodness but through God's relentless grace.

I

DÉJÀ VU ALL OVER AGAIN
(GENESIS 25:19–34)

In a few story lines of the popular *Peanuts* cartoon strip, Linus and Lucy have a little brother who goes by the name of Rerun. That's a really odd name, isn't it? I don't think that that was necessarily the name his parents gave him; perhaps it expresses Lucy's sense of disappointment in discovering that her second younger sibling is *another* boy. But there is a sense in which all of our children could legitimately be named Rerun, expressing the fact that in our children we see a reflection of ourselves. In many ways, their attributes and their skills, their strengths and their weaknesses, their interests and their passions—not to mention their looks—are often a rerun of our own. They are, as we might say, a chip off the old block.

A CHIP OFF THE OLD BLOCK

Isaac was, in the fullest sense of the phrase, a chip off the old block. In fact, the few events of his life that Scripture records for us are a great deal like his father's life. His life is, in Yogi Berra's memorable phrase, "déjà vu all over again." The result of this juxtaposition is that we can see clearly the ways in which he shared his father's strengths and weaknesses.

First, there was the same problem of a barren wife, threatening the fulfillment of God's promise of numerous descendants (Gen. 25:21). Then, like his father before him, he was faced with famine. God's promised land seemed unable to support him, and he had to decide whether to stay there or leave it for the perennially greener pastures of Egypt. In that situation of weakness, Isaac encountered the same temptation that his father had of passing off his wife as his sister in order to protect his life (Gen. 26:1–11). Subsequently he was involved in quarreling between his herdsmen and those of an ally, Abimelech, over scarce resources, a conflict that closely mirrors the earlier conflict between the herdsmen of Abraham and Abimelech (Gen. 26:12–35). Isaac's life is thus in a sense a rerun of the life of Abraham.

Isaac's life is not merely a compilation album of Abraham's greatest hits, however. Rather, in Isaac's replaying of Abraham's experience we also see God's faithfulness extended to a new generation. The promise to Abraham was valid for Isaac also. That surely was an important lesson for the original audience of the Book of Genesis, the wilderness generation, who stood with Moses on the brink of the Promised Land. They had not personally experienced the exodus out of Egypt; they had to rely on their fathers' testimony for that. Would the God who had done great things for their fathers also do great things for them, so that they might conquer the land? The answer was that just as Isaac could count on the God of Abraham, so also the God of Moses would continue to be with his people as they attempted to conquer the land under Joshua.

That is an important lesson for us and for our children as well. Like them, we too can rely on the God of Abraham and Isaac, the God of Moses and Joshua, to fulfill faithfully his promises to us in our day and situation. God does not change; his faithfulness endures forever.

REBEKAH'S BARRENNESS

The story of Isaac starts in Genesis 25:21 with Rebekah's barrenness. She was unable to bear children. This is a tragedy at any time, a pain that perhaps cannot be completely understood except by those going through it. Yet in Isaac and Rebekah's case the problem was worse. God's promise, after all, revolved around their having children, an uncountable multitude of descendants. Yet here they were, in the same boat in which Abraham and Sarah had found themselves forty years before. We are back face-to-face with the question that repeatedly faced Isaac's father, Abraham: Can God fulfill the promise in his strength, or does he need a little assistance from us to help him out?

During his lifetime, Abraham was presented with that choice over and over again, and slowly he learned to make the right choice. He found that it was one thing to "believe God and have it credited to him as righteousness" (Gen. 15:6) but quite another to move that belief from his head into his heart and trust God completely in the everyday decisions of life.

Perhaps that is where you find yourself. You have trusted God completely for your salvation, but you're not quite so sure about trusting him with the day-to-day decisions. How are you to find a wife or a husband? How are you to find a job? How are you to behave in a particularly difficult situation that faces you at work or in a relationship? The reality of our faith is daily put to a multitude of little (and not so little) tests. Of course, when what God has promised doesn't seem to be materializing, Satan is immediately on hand offering us deceptive shortcuts that seem at first sight to bring us to the same point. For Abraham and Sarah, as the years of waiting dragged on, he presented the shortcut of Hagar, Sarah's Egyptian maidservant (Gen. 16). It seemed to human wisdom a practical way of bringing about the desired result. The result, however, was disaster. The child who was produced by this strategy was not Isaac, the child of promise, but Ishmael.

In so many situations, the choice that faces us is essentially the same as that which faced the patriarchs: believe God, even when it doesn't seem likely to work, or follow Satan's shortcut. So how does Isaac respond to his testing situation? He is a model of faith. He prayed to the Lord for Rebekah; the Lord answered his prayer, and she became pregnant (Gen. 25:21).

The text makes it sound so easy, doesn't it? Isaac prayed, and God gave him the desires of his heart. It is only when you get to Genesis 25:26 that you discover that it wasn't quite as straightforward as that. Like Abraham and Sarah before them, Isaac and Rebekah waited a long time to see their prayers answered, twenty years in all. Year after year went by, and nothing seemed to be happening. But unlike Abraham and Sarah, there was no tension in the wait for Isaac and Rebekah. They had learned from Abraham and Sarah's example that God could be trusted. So they waited with such patience that there is nothing much to report between the praying of the prayer and its answer. There was no Hagar for them. Satan's shortcuts were of no interest to Isaac and Rebekah. They believed God and were willing to leave the outcome to him. With such an attitude, it sometimes turns out that the longest-delayed answers to prayer are the most faith-building, because when they are finally answered we see in them most clearly the hand of God.

DEALING WITH DISAPPOINTMENT

But what if God should see fit not to give us in this life what we earnestly seek from him? What if even after long years of waiting, we are still disappointed? God is, after all, not the great slot machine in the sky, whose arm you twist until you hit the jackpot and he gives you the desires of your heart. He is not the custodian of a celestial warehouse of delights waiting for you to dial the right number so that he can release your personal prize pack of blessings.

He is nonetheless good. He gives us that which we most need. Has he not given us Jesus, his beloved Son? Will he not give us eternal life in his presence? If we have that, then what of real significance do we lack? To complain, as we so often do, that he has failed to give us this or that earthly good gift, though we sought it from him with earnest prayer and tears, is like a toddler fussing on Christmas Day because the large pile of presents he received did not come wrapped in the particular paper he wanted. God's goodness to his people has been demonstrated beyond question in the death of Jesus for us on the cross. This reality remains true, even though he should ask us to follow a similar path of suffering and self-denial during our earthly pilgrimage to the one our Savior trod before us.

I recently sat with a woman who had been suffering from cancer for ten years. She had at times been paralyzed by the effects of the cancer and was now in excruciating pain from the course of treatment she was undergoing. The pain was so intense that she had not slept for several nights. What responses could I give her for the natural questions: Why, Lord? How long will I have to endure this pain? Why can't you be glorified by healing me, instead of making me continue to suffer? There are no simple answers. But there is the promise of God to be with us in and through it all, and the assurance that nothing in all creation—neither death, nor life, nor sickness nor health, nor riches nor poverty—nothing can separate us from the love of God (see Rom. 8:38–39). We will often have to live by faith in that statement rather than by sight, as to outward appearances it is hardly self-evident. But as we tread the hard road by faith, we can look back again and again to the cross where that love was demonstrated for all to see, once and for all time.

TURMOIL WITHIN

Finally the long years of waiting seemed about to come to an end for Isaac and Rebekah. Rebekah discovered that she was expecting the double blessing of twins (Gen. 25:22). Even before the twins were born, though, there seemed to be some family disharmony. It is illuminating to contrast the first appearances of Abraham and Jacob onto the stage of biblical history. When we first meet Abraham, he is seventy-five years old and about to step out in faith. When we first meet Jacob, he's not even born and already he's involved in a struggle with his brother, Esau. He is born grabbing his brother's heel, either trying to overtake him or to trip him up. In many ways, that first encounter sets the stage for all that will follow, for Abraham and Jacob. Abraham shows us faith in human form, journeying toward the Promised Land. Jacob, the man stumbling from one family conflict to another, demonstrates quite a different virtue. He shows us the triumph of grace over all obstacles. Jacob, with all of his sinning, scheming, and plotting, is the perfect model of how God's undeserved favor can succeed even with the most unpromising material.

When Rebekah sought to find out why this turmoil was taking place inside her, she was given an oracle from the Lord:

> Two nations are in your womb,
>   and two peoples from within you will be
>   separated;
> one people will be stronger than the other,
>   and the older will serve the younger.
>   (Gen. 25:23)

This revelation made it clear to her that this was not just a routine brotherly squabble, such as happens even in the best of families. Rather, there were two future nations involved. What is more, God was going to reverse the usual pattern of things: the older would serve the younger.

This theme of conflict between brothers or within families is not new at this point in Genesis. Such a struggle was evident already between Cain and Abel in Genesis 4; there too the younger child turned out to be the one who bore God's favor. Throughout the rest of the Book of Genesis, there is a series of family conflicts. From the sons of Noah, through Abraham and Lot, Isaac and Ishmael, Jacob and Laban, and on down to Joseph and his brothers, there is a constant pattern of rivalry and discord within the family. And the ultimate reason for all such discord is election. Those whom God has not chosen, or who are living out of step with God, are always at war with those whom God has chosen, even when they grow up within the same household. But out of those struggles, God's purposes to bless his people stand secure. Though the seed of the serpent do its worst, it cannot prevail against the power of the living God. As Genesis 50:20 articulates it, "You intended to harm me, but God intended it for good."

THE OLDER SHALL SERVE THE YOUNGER

Repeatedly the pattern emerges that "the older will serve the younger" (Gen. 25:23). Abel was accepted while Cain was rejected; the line of Seth was chosen over the line of Cain; Isaac is chosen over Ishmael, Rachel over her older sister, Leah, and Joseph over all his older brothers. Why does God act in this way? Paul lays out the reasons for us in Romans 9:10–12:

> Rebekah's children had one and the same father, our father Isaac. Yet, before the twins were born or had done anything good or bad—in order that God's purpose in election might stand: not by works but by him who calls—she was told, "The older will serve the younger."

God wants to make it clear from the start that there is no favoritism with him. There are no privileged positions. Being born of Abraham is not enough; being born of Isaac and Rebekah is not enough; being the oldest child is not enough. God will have mercy on whom he will have mercy, and he will harden whom he will harden. Our salvation is all of grace, not of our merit. God is no respecter of persons. He chooses the foolish things of the world to shame the wise; he chooses the weak things of the world to shame the strong. He chooses the unfavored younger sons to show that all is of grace from start to finish.

In the context of everything Isaac and Rebekah knew about God and God's purposes, what did the oracle mean? What did it mean to say that "the younger will serve the older"? Surely it should have been clear to them that this was God's way of telling them that the promised Savior would come of the line of the younger. In order once again to show God's absolute sovereignty in salvation, God would choose not only the family through whom the promise would come but even how the promise descended in that family. What should have happened, then, was that as the boys grew up they should have been prepared for their destinies in God's plan. Esau should have been prepared for his need to find a blessing in Jacob and particularly in Jacob's descendant through whom salvation would come. Jacob should have been prepared for his role as godly ancestor of the Messiah, recognizing in humility that he had been given a high calling not because of his greatness but through God's choosing. How much family disharmony might have been avoided if God's words had been heeded!

But that did not happen. Instead of being trained for God's calling, the boys were allowed to develop in their own ways. Esau was the strong one, the outdoors type, good at hunting, gifted at life in the field. He is, after all, the original redneck, as he is described at the time of his birth: he was ruddy in complexion and thoroughly hairy (Gen. 25:25). When you think of Esau, think pickup trucks, ponytails, and tattoos. Just as in our culture, in the ancient Near East excessive hairiness was a feature generally associated with boorish and uncouth behavior.

As for Jacob, the text describes him by the deliberately ambiguous Hebrew word *tam* (Gen. 25:27). This word has caused the English translations some difficulty. It means essentially "single-minded" or "single-hearted" and thus usually has positive overtones describing a man of high moral character. It describes someone whose desires and actions are thoroughly integrated, as does the root of the English word *integrity.* In Jacob's case, however, his single-mindedness would lead him in a less positive direction, as we shall see. What is more, unlike his brother, his natural habitat was the tent, not the field. Once again there is a certain ambiguity in that description. It could describe his occupation as a (civilized) nomadic shepherd rather than as a hunter like his brother. But in what follows, his perpetual presence in the tent is also crucial to his efforts to rob his brother of his birthright. Because of his passion for staying at home, he was able to be in the right place at the right time to pursue his single-minded schemes.

The differences between the boys also led to the poisonous presence of favoritism on the part of the parents. Genesis 25:28 holds a warning that every parent should take seriously to heart:

> Isaac, who had a taste for wild game, loved Esau, but Rebekah loved Jacob.

Not only is there favoritism here, but also the children were valued for what they could do for the parents. Isaac, who had a taste for wild game, loved Esau. The text doesn't tell us why Rebekah loved Jacob. Perhaps she remembered the oracle concerning him. Or perhaps it was his propensity for hanging around the tents where she was. Children are all different in their temperaments: some are sporty and outgoing, others are shy bookworms. Some are passionately musical or artistic, while others prefer surfing the Internet or tearing apart a car engine. How easy it would be to love those best whose interests and aptitudes are closest to ours. How easy, but how terrible in its consequences! The ground was being prepared by the parents for a lifetime of strife between the children. In time, the sin of Isaac and Rebekah would come home to roost in a fitting judgment of God: Isaac would be deceived by his taste for wild game, while Rebekah would find her stay-at-home son propelled far away from her.

LET'S MAKE A DEAL

It is the boys' respective aptitudes that form the backdrop for the next scene. They had been doing what they did best. Esau had been out in the fields hunting and came home famished. The pickup skidded to a halt outside the tent. When he went inside, he found that Jacob had made a pot of his favorite lentil soup. Immediately he wanted to have some (Gen. 25:29–30). There nothing unusual or wrong with that; it happens in the best of families. Just how dysfunctional this particular family was, however, can be seen from what follows. In a situation like that, most people would say, "Here, brother, draw up a stool and help yourself." What Jacob said to Esau, though, was, "First sell me your birthright" (Gen. 25:31). What is more, even when Esau made what sounded like a verbal commitment to do so in response,

Jacob was not content with that. He demanded further that Esau swear an oath, dragging the name of the Lord into this shoddy enterprise.

What was Jacob doing? He was taking Satan's short-cut. He was not willing to wait for God to fulfill the promise that "the older shall serve the younger" in God's time. Instead, Jacob wanted to snatch it for himself now by his cleverness. Equally, of course, Esau should not have agreed to any such deal. He should have preferred to eat a crust of dry bread than willingly give up his birthright, the expectation that, humanly speaking, *his* should have been the line to bear the promised Messiah. He counted that privilege of less value than a bowl of soup.

What makes it all worse is the fact that, in spite of his protestations, this was hardly a matter of life or death for Esau (Gen. 25:32). He was not going to die if he didn't get the soup. This was rather a matter of a man driven by his appetites to exchange what is of eternal value for a brief moment's pleasure. He didn't even linger to savor the culinary experience. He gulped his food down and was gone without a thought for what he had left behind. But before you and I judge him too quickly for that, do we not do the same? Is there some cherished sin that you are unwilling to part with for the sake of the kingdom? Is there some appetite, some momentary pleasure that you count of greater weight than the kingdom of God? How many people have made shipwreck of their careers, their reputations, and their lives in pursuit of a moment's satisfaction? We too have often placed little or no value on the privilege of being called God's children. Let those who are without sin in this area cast the first stone.

DESPISING THE BIRTHRIGHT

So Esau despised his birthright (Gen. 25:34). It was fitting, therefore, that that which he despised should ultimately be taken from him. God's choice of Jacob over Esau is seen to be in no sense unfair, because it merely takes from him something that he counts of no value. That is how the process of election always works. Those who remain outside God's kingdom, who have not received his election and calling to become part of his people, do not lose something they sought to have but rather something they counted of no value. Noah does not have to fight to keep the masses out of the ark, as if it were the last lifeboat to leave a sinking ship. He does not have to stand by the gangplank with a shotgun, warding off the crowds. In fact, quite the reverse: only those whose hearts God has changed would want to take shelter within its confining walls.

Isn't this what we see all around us? There are multitudes who have no real interest in God and his way of salvation, even as they pursue all kinds of other spiritual paths. God continues to choose and call those who are his, but those who are passed over by God will never complain that God is being unfair. Left to themselves, they have no desire to be chosen.

Perhaps we may think of it in these terms. Imagine the government were to hold a drawing to select the first team of citizen astronauts. Social Security numbers would be selected at random to identify a group of ordinary citizens to take part in the national space program. Those selected would endure a rigorous training program but would be assured a place in history—ultimate glory, we might say. Some people might clamor to be among those chosen, but others, myself included, would be content to be passed by for that particular glory. I would not complain about being left out because the prize for participation holds no strong attraction. In the same way, only those whose hearts God has laid hold of and brought to desire his glory and his approval above all things will long to spend eternity with him. For the others, such a birthright holds little attraction.

But woe to him through whom the temptation to sell the birthright comes! Once again, as elsewhere in Genesis, temptation comes to Esau through those most closely related to him. Jacob willingly becomes Satan's instrument to tempt his brother; he ultimately pays a terrible price for taking Satan's shortcut. He will gain the birthright by one stratagem or another, but it will be a very long time before he is free to enjoy it. Unlike Isaac and Rebekah earlier in this chapter, Jacob is not willing to wait patiently for God to do what he has promised. He wants that blessing, and he wants it *now!* Perhaps you too know that temptation. You desire to see God's healing, or for God to give you a spouse, or a child, or to deliver you from a really tough situation. It is appropriate to have those longings and to pray for God to act in your life. But if you have to have it *now,* then beware. You are in danger of desiring the blessing more than you desire God, and when that happens you may be easy prey for Satan to offer you a shortcut.

Invariably Satan's shortcuts don't work. They may be short, but they don't take you where you want to go. They promise much and deliver little. They promise a shortcut into the Promised Land but leave you with another forty years to wander in the wilderness. They promise an easy way to acquire the blessing but leave you running for your life. Obedience may seem like the hard choice at the time. Leaving everything to God in faith may seem ever so difficult, but it is far easier in the long run, as Abraham, Isaac, and Jacob each found. Living by faith may not be the easy way, but it is ultimately the only way to live at peace with God and with those around you.

THE SAVIOR JACOB NEEDS

What is God to do with such a pair? One of them regards his spiritual birthright as less valuable than a bowl of soup, and the other regards it as a commodity to be bought and maneuvered for. Which of these two should God choose to save? A neutral bystander would have to say neither. Neither one deserves God's work in his heart. What clearer evidence could there be that God's calculations are not the same as ours? What more proof do we need that our salvation is all of grace?

But how can God save such great sinners? There is only one hope. He must send a savior who is unlike Jacob and Esau. He must send a savior who would regard his birthright, that of being equal with God and receiving the eternal praise of the heavenly hosts in heaven, as something he would not grasp greedily but would freely give up for others. He must send a savior who would happily don a servant's towel and not only cook for his disciples but perform an even more menial task for them, that of washing their feet. He must send a savior who regarded the birthright of his chosen people, which we despised and trampled underfoot, as so precious that he would gladly purchase it at a price not measurable in gold or silver: the cost of his blood. Such is the Savior Jacob needs. Only the irresistible grace of God can cover his sin and self-centeredness. Such is the Savior we need. Only the irresistible grace of God can cover my sin and self-centeredness. Thanks be to God, such is the Savior he has provided for us in Jesus!

FOR FURTHER REFLECTION

1. Why is it significant that Isaac's life is parallel in so many ways to Abraham's life?
2. What did Isaac do when God's promises seemed unlikely to be fulfilled in his life? In what areas of your life are you tempted to doubt the likelihood of God fulfilling his promises?
3. What is the key to learning to wait patiently?

4. Why does God reverse the natural order and choose Jacob? Is it because of anything in Jacob? Why is this aspect of God's character good news for us?

5. In what ways are Jacob and Esau wrong in the incident of the bowl of soup? How might we as Christians despise our birthright? How might we seek to manipulate God into giving us blessings?

6. How do Jacob and Esau point us to Jesus as the answer to our need of a savior?

2

PATRIARCH II:
SON OF ABRAHAM
(GENESIS 26)

The makers of movies over the past twenty years or so have had a passion for sequels. Not content with *Rocky*, they have given us *Rocky II, Rocky III, Rocky IV*, and so on. In a similar way, *Jurassic Park* begets two more movies in its own likeness, as does *Beethoven*. A true sequel of this kind often involves not only the same characters but also the same basic plot structure. From Hollywood's perspective, this approach saves a lot of time and effort in scriptwriting, not to mention the hard work of coming up with an original idea.

We have already noticed the fact that Isaac's life is, in many ways, this kind of sequel to the life of Abraham, a sequel that shares plot structure and themes. We might aptly title the movie of his life *Patriarch II: Son of Abraham*. Yet the Bible's goal in this approach is not to save time and money, nor does it stem from a lack of original ideas on the part of the author. The same themes are being deliberately reiterated in the experience of Isaac to emphasize the central message of the life of Abraham, that God can be trusted to deliver what he has promised, and to show how those promises continue to be operative in the life of the next generation.

The replaying of Abraham's experiences in the life of Isaac continues to be prominent in Genesis 26. First, father and son had shared the experience of a barren wife; now they shared the experience of a barren land (Gen. 26:1). The Promised Land was once more racked with famine, a similarity that the aside of verse 1—"besides the earlier famine of Abraham's time"—underlines. Isaac was faced with the same temptation to abandon the promise and go down to the abundant prosperity of Egypt, just as his father did before him.

At the critical juncture, however, the Lord appeared to Isaac and told him not to take the high road to Egypt (Gen. 26:2). Rather, he should stay where he is, in spite of the famine. The Lord promised to fulfill his oath to Abraham and give him land and offspring and blessing. Faced with a choice between the apparent foolishness of trusting God and the wisdom of choosing with his eyes, Isaac once again passed the test with flying colors. By faith, he resisted that temptation to flee to Egypt on the strength of the bare word of God's promise. If you like, he too believed God, and it was reckoned to him as righteousness. It looks as if the moral of the story would be that the children have learned their lesson from the sins of their father.

But immediately after he had received from the Lord a renewal of the covenant made with his father and imitated his father's faith in the covenant-keeping God, Isaac proceeded to imitate also his father's propensity for fudging. The issue was a situation that had parallels to that of Abraham. Living as an alien in the land of Gerar, Isaac was without legal rights or recourse. The possibility of violence against him from the inhabitants of the land was ever present, and he feared for his life. More precisely, Isaac was afraid that if good-looking Rebekah were recognized as his wife, his life would be in danger (Gen.

26:7). He feared that he would meet with a convenient accident to free Rebekah for marriage, a fear that was far from being irrational or unfounded. Under those circumstances, he decided that he would rather risk giving up his wife than giving up his life.

The fundamental issue at stake here is a familiar one: Can God be trusted to fulfill his promises and protect Isaac? God had just promised to be with Isaac, giving him offspring, lands, and blessing (Gen. 26:4). So there was no question as to God's commitment to him. The question was whether Isaac has the faith to believe God and let the chips fall where they may or adopt a strategy of deception to give God a little assistance.

In this case, like his father before him, Isaac gave in to the temptation to speak misleading half-truths to protect himself. Looking after his life had become more important to him than obeying God. The irony is that the God whom he is so reluctant to trust with his life is the same God who provided a lamb to take his place on the altar of Mount Moriah. If God was able to deliver Isaac's life from the upraised knife of his father, would he not also deliver Isaac from the dangers of everyday life in a pagan society? Had he learned nothing from that experience? But before we judge Isaac too harshly, we need to examine our hearts. How often do you and I fail to obey God when something far less significant than our lives is at stake? We frequently choose the way of self-protective deception for the sake of mere comfort or pleasure or reputation, forgetting the love of God demonstrated in the Lamb he provided to take our place on the cross of Calvary. If God did not spare his Son but freely gave him up for us, can we not trust him with our lives? What weak and fickle people we are!

But Isaac was wrong about God, and it turned out that he was also wrong about those around him. He lived unmolested there in Gerar for a long time before his subterfuge was finally uncovered. Unlike his father's experience, Rebekah was never in danger of being lost into the harem of the king. But when Abimelech caught him engaged in the kind of behavior that is not normally undertaken with one's sister (Gen. 26:8) and asked him to explain himself, Isaac's answer was revealing. He replied, "*I* thought *I* might lose my life" (Gen. 26:9). The pronouns are precisely the problem: he was thinking only of himself, not of the damage his actions might do to others. The possibility that others might be taken in by his subterfuge and bring guilt upon themselves by taking Rebekah as a wife apparently never crossed his mind. Equally, he apparently never considered the possibility that this Abimelech, presumably a descendant of the Abimelech with whom his father had dealings in Genesis 20, might turn out to be an honorable and God-fearing man. He neglected the possibility that God could work for good even in the lives of the pagans around him.

FORGETTING TO FEAR GOD

Isn't that so often the root of our sin? We're driven by what *we* want, by what would make *us* comfortable, by what would make *us* safe, and we don't think about others. When you opt out of sharing the gospel with someone, how often is it because you fear feeling uncomfortable? But what about the guilt that rests upon that person that only the gospel can cleanse away? Have you thought of that? Or are you thinking only of yourself? Perhaps you think to yourself that it is unlikely that someone like them could believe and be saved. Have you forgotten the mighty power of God that he exercised in your life when he drew you to himself? Is it impossible for him to do the same work in the heart of the one whom you fear, no matter how unlikely that may appear on a human level? Is anything too hard for God?

It is also noticeable that when Isaac stopped fearing

God and putting obedience to God first, he started fearing everyone else. As long as he was fearing God, he had nothing to fear from any man or woman, and so he was free to go out and serve others with boldness. When he started thinking only about himself, however, and about trying to protect himself, he ceased thinking about others and caring for them. He was no longer free to serve; instead, he was locked into trying to protect himself. It's an insidious shift, and it can happen so easily to us all. As I have been thinking about this passage, I've also become aware that I've been putting off a difficult but necessary phone call. Because I've been fearing others, I haven't been free to be a blessing to them.

What is the answer for our self-protectiveness? The answer is the gospel. We need to remind ourselves over and over again of Jesus, the one who did not fear men, who did not economize on the truth to save himself. Though the truth about who he was remained veiled while he was on earth, it was not veiled for the sake of his safety. On the contrary, it was veiled so that he might lay down his life for the sake of his people, bearing the servant's form that he had taken upon himself all the way to the cross. His thought was not of himself and his comfort and safety. His focus was entirely upon the glory of God that would be demonstrated in the saving of an unrighteous, unworthy people and restoring them into a holy nation. Nor was this plan limited to the children of Abraham. His work included the bringing of Gentiles like Abimelech into the inheritance in the one kingdom of God alongside covenant-breaking sons of Abraham, such as Isaac, so that God's salvation might extend to the ends of the earth. As God declared to the servant of the Lord through the prophet Isaiah:

> It is too small a thing for you to be my servant
> to restore the tribes of Jacob
> and bring back those of Israel I have kept.

I will also make you a light for the Gentiles,
that you may bring my salvation to the ends
of the earth. (Isa. 49:6)

Knowing and fearing this God gives you the power to be free of any other fears in this life, for if this God is with us, who can be against us?

GOD'S FAITHFUL PRESENCE

God was with Isaac as he had promised. In spite of Isaac's sin and failure, God was nonetheless faithful. His blessing rested upon Isaac, and he became rich. He reaped a hundredfold what he sowed and became materially prosperous, even in a time of famine (Gen. 26:12–13). However, material blessings always bring problems and difficulties with them. Just like his father before him, Isaac found that prosperity can be as big a test as poverty (see Gen. 13:5–7). The Philistines, among whom Isaac was living, became jealous of his prosperity and started to harass him, blocking up the wells he needed for his flocks and herds and eventually asking him to move away from their land (Gen. 26:15–16). His life became one of constant conflict and forced wandering.

Why was God seemingly giving with one hand and taking away with the other? Isaac was once more being put to the test. He was discovering that he, like his father before him, was nothing more than an alien and a stranger in the Promised Land. He was thereby forced to recognize that God's ultimate blessing upon him must rest in something other and more than material prosperity. There was more to God's covenant with Abraham than ownership of a piece of earthly real estate. Far from possessing the land, Isaac found himself evicted from part of it by the present occupants. Far from the nations of the earth coming to bless themselves in his offspring, as God had promised in Genesis 26:4, the nations at present seemed far more inclined to curse him as a nuisance. Each time his servants dug out one of the old wells that dated back to the days of Abraham, the Philistines came and took it away from them (Gen. 26:18–21). That is so often the way life is in a fallen world. Rich though Isaac was, there was still a wide gap between what God had promised and the reality that Isaac experienced, just as there had been for his father, Abraham.

The persistent conflict with the Philistines might easily have worn Isaac down and caused him to doubt the promise. Instead, he persevered, until at last he found a well that no one would quarrel over. When he did so, he significantly named it Rehoboth ("space"), with a declaration of faith: "Now the LORD has given us room and we will be fruitful in the land" (Gen. 26:22). The mandate of God for humanity in the beginning was to be fruitful and fill the land (Gen. 1:28); now Isaac declared that the Lord has given his new humanity a place where that word may be fulfilled. Subsequently at Beersheba, the Lord appeared to him again, confirming the promise, and Isaac built an altar there and worshiped him (Gen. 26:24–25). His faith was rewarded by fellowship with his God.

THE FRUITS OF PEACE

Isaac's efforts to live at peace with his neighbors did in the end bear earthly as well as heavenly fruit, however. After all this had transpired, Abimelech came to make a covenant with Isaac at Beersheba, the same place where his ancestor had earlier made a covenant with Abraham (Gen. 26:26; see Gen. 21:22–24). That is as it should be. If we are living our lives properly, there should be something attractive about our lives as the people of God. According to the Bible, people should recognize us as Christians by our love, not by our long faces. We should not be known as grumblers and troublemakers but as peacemakers. Even on an earthly level, we should be the kind of neighbors that people long for, not the kind they dread. As Paul puts it:

> Do not repay anyone evil for evil. Be careful to do what is right in the eyes of everybody. If it is possible, as far as it depends on you, live at peace with everyone. (Rom. 12:17–18)

Isaac demonstrates clearly the principle of not repaying evil for evil. One suspects that his eyebrows might have lifted a touch at Abimelech's claim that he had "always treated you well and sent you away in peace" (Gen. 26:29). He may have been tempted to respond, "That's not how I remember it!" and to reopen some of the quarrels from earlier in the chapter. But if so, he resisted the temptation. He had learned the lesson that Proverbs 19:11 teaches:

> A man's wisdom gives him patience;
> > it is to his glory to overlook an offense.

However, there is more to this covenant between Isaac and Abimelech than an example of wise behavior. The writer of the Book of Genesis wants us to see more than a man at peace with the people who live next door. He wants us to see the promise that God made to Abraham in Genesis 12:3 being fulfilled, the promise that God had reiterated to Isaac in Genesis 26:4. God had promised that the nations would come and find a blessing for themselves in Abraham and his descendants. There is peace to be found in relationship to Abraham and his seed, a peace that foreshadows and points to the peace to be found in relationship to the ultimate son of Abraham, Jesus Christ. Supremely it is to him that all must come to find peace.

What was it that drew Abimelech to Isaac? It was this: "We saw clearly that the LORD was with you" (Gen. 26:28). By his lifestyle, by his peaceable nature, by the blessing of God that self-evidently rested upon him, Isaac demonstrated the fundamental truth of Immanuel, God with us. His life pointed people to the God with whom he walked. He pointed people to the one to come, whose very name would be Immanuel ("God is with us"), because he *was* God in human form, God with us to make peace between God and us. Jesus did not come to bring us earthly prosperity but every spiritual blessing in him (Eph. 1:3). He came not merely to give us space to live and a well that we could call our own but rather living water that would flow out from us to the nations, drawing men and women to faith in him through our witness (John 7:38). Could it be said of your lifestyle that "we see clearly that God is with you"? Does your daily walk point people unmistakably to the God whom you serve and whose presence in your life you claim? Is there a blessing that flows out from you to those who surround you?

But in the case of Jesus, there was no nonaggression pact between him and the nations. Far from it, the nations conspired together with his people to put him to death on a cross. But even this was part of God's sovereign purpose to bring his chosen ones to himself, to unite together into one body Jews and Gentiles (Acts 4:27–28). So also for us, a righteous lifestyle will not always result in trouble-free relationships with those around us. The other side of Paul's admonition to live at peace with our neighbors is his sobering caution to Timothy:

> In fact, everyone who wants to live a godly life in Christ Jesus will be persecuted. (2 Tim. 3:12)

Even in the midst of persecution, however, our peace, gentleness, and patience may still point people to our God.

MARRYING THE WORLD

After the high point of Isaac's covenant of peace, however, which resulted in a renewed naming of the site of the future town of Beersheba, Genesis 26 closes on a negative note. Isaac had demonstrated the proper way of relating to those around him: living in peace, by faith, in order to point them to the God who is with us. As a result, he received God's rich blessing. Esau, however, proceeded to demonstrate the wrong way of relating to those around us who aren't believers: marrying them. The extraordinary care that Abraham took to make sure that Isaac would find a spiritually suitable bride was of no consequence to Esau. He had no thought of spiritual things, of the Promised Land, of living by faith as a stranger and an alien in this world. Instead, ironically at the same age at which his father married Rebekah, Esau married himself to this world, acquiring not one but two pagan wives (Gen. 26:34). Thus he became a source of great grief to his parents.

There must be a distinctiveness about you as a Christian if you are to fulfill your God-given role of drawing the world to Christ. There must be a saltiness that makes you different from the world. You are to be in the world but not of it. You should stand out as different in your workplace and in your neighborhood. Isaac, for all his imperfections, was such a person. He was spiritually as well as physically a true son of Abraham. Jacob, at least by the time God had finished with him, was also going to be such a person. Esau, however, was not a son of Abraham in the spiritual sense, and he never would be. Thus we are coming to see working itself out in the lives of Esau and Jacob what God had sovereignly declared before they were born: that his sovereign choice for salvation rested on the younger, not the older.

ELECTION: SOVEREIGN BUT NOT ARBITRARY

The doctrine of election is a difficult one for many people. They struggle with the justice of the idea that God chooses some for salvation and passes over others. Some people, therefore, have argued that it is a matter of God's foreknowledge. God knows in advance which people are going to choose him, and therefore he responds by choosing them. The Bible, however, is clear. God's love for his chosen people existed long before their birth, all the way back to the foundation of the world (Eph. 1:4–5). God does not love us because he foresaw we would love him. Rather, we love God because he loved us from the first (1 John 4:10). In this way, our salvation is seen to rest on God's mercy and not on anything in us (Rom. 9:16).

Yet, as we pointed out earlier, even though God's election is sovereign, it is not arbitrary and unjust. It is not as if Esau desperately wanted to be a chosen son and God harshly turned him away, not allowing him a place among his chosen people. No, Esau has twice turned his back on his spiritual birthright. First, he sold his birthright to his brother for a bowl of lentil soup (Gen. 25:31–34). Now he compromised the fundamental goal of God's election: the creation of a separate, holy people for God. Under the circumstances, Esau could have no complaints about being passed over.

We should also notice, however, that Jacob is not chosen because, in contrast to Esau, he is such a wonderful person. Jacob shows himself to be a scheming, conniving, calculating little rat, especially during the first part of his life. Nonetheless, because God's choice rests upon him out of his sovereign mercy, God is going to work on Jacob, reshaping him, purifying him into a person he can use. Neither Jacob nor Esau deserves God's grace in his life, but God's sovereign mercy rests upon Jacob for his blessing, and so his grace begins the transforming work in his heart.

So it is also for us. Our election and our salvation are entirely of grace. God did not choose you because you were better or smarter or more beautiful or holier than everyone else. God did not choose you because he foresaw that you would exercise faith while others wouldn't. God chose us while we were still filthy sinners, because of his electing grace. Even with his transforming power at work in our hearts, though, the best of saints make only small beginnings on the path of holy living. We never outgrow our need for grace while we live on earth.

But God's sovereign choice in salvation is not arbitrary. Those passed over by God have no cause for complaint. Their condemnation is thoroughly deserved. Even though we plead with them with tears to abandon their self-destructive course and find salvation in Jesus Christ, they will have none of it. The whole idea is foolishness to them. Those whom God chooses, he then begins to reshape into a people for his pleasure. As Ephesians 1:4 puts it, "He chose us . . . to be holy and blameless in his sight." The result is that those chosen have no cause for arrogance. Their justification is undeserved by them. It is merited only by the righteousness of Christ that is credited to their account, and it is worked in them by the indwelling power of the Holy Spirit. All is of God, so that God may receive all the glory.

That truth should give us boldness in our sharing of the gospel. We may freely call all who will to come to Jesus and be saved. The invitation to the party is open to all. Whoever you are, whatever you have done, your sins too can be paid for by the death of Jesus on the cross. No one is too guilty or too defiled to come. You too can receive Christ's righteousness credited to your account. You too can participate in the feast that God has prepared for

all who are his people on the final day. It's a genuine offer, and we pray fervently and intently that many people
will respond to it in faith. But we trust the outcome of our
evangelism to the care of a good God, who chose a people who would be his before the foundation of the world.

That too is a comforting thought, given the imperfec-
tion of so much of our gospel witness. It is God who de-
termines the outcome of our speaking for him, not the
quality of our speech. It is God's choice whether our
words fall on the ears of an Esau, to whom they are all
nonsense, or on the ears of a Jacob, for whom the road to
faith may be long and hard but will eventually bring him
to glory. It is God's choice whether our words fall on the
ears of an Abraham who is ready now to hear and trust
and believe. We therefore invite all to come to Christ to receive the living water from him, confident that all those
whom the Lord our God is calling to himself will hear his
voice and will come. To him indeed will be all the glory.

This truth should also give us great joy in the midst of
our manifold sins and failures. Do you know yourself to be
a sinner in God's sight? Are there areas of your life where
you continue to fail God over and over again? If so, the bad
news is that you are normal. But the good news is that if
God has laid hold on you by his electing grace, he will sus-
tain you by that grace through every step of your earthly
journey. He will use even that sin which you find so difficult to combat as a means of driving you back to the cross.
And one day, at the end of all things, you too will be purified completely by his grace and will stand before him
without fault or blemish. What a wonderful, heartwarm-
ing, comforting doctrine the doctrine of God's election is!

FOR FURTHER REFLECTION

1. How do we know that we can trust God to do what
    is best for us? When do we most need to know that?

2. How do you see God at work for your good in the lives of pagans around you? How can you bring blessing into their lives?
3. Why is prosperity such a big test for us? How can we resist the temptations that it brings?
4. In what ways do you see the temptation in your life to marry the world?
5. Why is it important that God's election is not arbitrary? Why is it encouraging to know that God's election is the decisive factor in salvation?

3

WHO'S TO BLAME?

(GENESIS 27)

I remember when I was a boy being an avid reader of a newspaper called the *Sunday Post*. It was a Scottish paper, so growing up in England I didn't get to see it every week. But our relatives north of the Border would save issues for us, and every few months we would receive a large stack to read. By then the news was always out of date, but nobody ever read the *Sunday Post* for its news anyway. What we enjoyed in the *Sunday Post* were the cartoons, the funny stories, and the features, and none of these became dated with the passage of time.

One of those features that I still remember was entitled "Who's to blame?" Each week it would feature a diagram of a traffic accident, showing little cars labeled A, B, and C with a brief description of what had happened. You had to decide whose fault the accident was, and then you could compare your answer with the official answer, given by a traffic policeman. The enduring popularity of that feature in our household stemmed from a basic feature of the human heart. Whenever something goes wrong, we always want to find someone whose fault it is. Whether the occurrence is as minor as a fender bender or as major as an unexpected death in the hospital, we are eager to find out who the guilty party is. We instinctively seek someone to blame.

In real life, however, the answer to such a question is often complex. The blame can rarely simply be assigned to A, B, or C alone. Frequently the more appropriate answer is "all of the above." For instance, who was to blame for humankind's first sin in the Garden of Eden? Was it Adam's fault for failing to keep the serpent out of the garden and then standing silently beside Eve while the serpent deceived her (Gen. 3:6)? After all, he had been assigned by God the task of guarding the garden. Or was it Eve's fault, as Adam was so quick to suggest (Gen. 3:12)? Was it really the serpent's fault, as Eve suggested (Gen. 3:13)? No, as God makes clear in his judgment, all were at fault.

Yet even out of that sordid scene in the garden comes a message of hope. God's purposes for man's ultimate good will stand; they cannot be frustrated by human failures. This is a tremendously important biblical principle: your sin, even while it may have real and lasting earthly consequences, cannot derail God's gracious purpose for your life. This principle of God's goodness and firm purpose enduring in spite of, and even through, human sinfulness, is evidenced once again in and through the sorry sight of family disharmony that we encounter in Genesis 27.

PASSING ON THE BLESSING

Isaac had by now grown old. He felt that it was time for him to pass on to his offspring the blessing God had given to his father, Abraham. God had promised Abraham that he would become a great nation, one through whom great blessing would come to all peoples (Gen. 12:1–3). God had promised him descendants as numerous as the stars of the sky (Gen. 15:5) and the land of Canaan for those descendants to dwell in (Gen. 17:8). Best of all, he promised to be Abraham's God and the God of his descendants after him (Gen. 17:8). The promise of these blessings had been repeated to Isaac (Gen. 26:24). Now, in spite of the oracle given at the birth of his sons, which declared that the older son would serve the younger, Isaac wished to pass on that blessing to Esau, his firstborn and favorite son. To that end, Esau was sent off to do what he did best as a "man of the open country" (Gen. 25:27): he was to hunt wild game and then make Isaac's favorite stew. This tasty stew was a key reason why Isaac loved Esau best (Gen. 25:28).

But Rebekah overheard Isaac's plan and set in motion a counterplan. Her goal was to win the blessing for her favorite son, Jacob. Taking advantage of the old man's blindness, she dressed Jacob in a makeshift outfit combining Esau's best clothes with goatskins to cover up Jacob's general lack of hairiness. Jacob at first objected, not so much out of moral scruples as out of concern that the plan might not work and he might bring down upon his head a curse rather than a blessing (Gen. 27:11). Once reassured on that score, he went in to his father dressed as his brother (Gen. 27:16). He presented to his father the stew that Rebekah had swiftly conjured up, and Jacob thoroughly deceived him.

Not only could Isaac's weakened sight not tell the brothers apart; even his other senses let him down. His sense of touch could not distinguish between Esau and the disguised Jacob (Gen. 27:22). His sense of smell was deceived by the scent of Esau's clothes in which Jacob was dressed (Gen. 27:27). Even his taste buds could not discern between the food his wife prepared and that of Esau (Gen. 27:25). This is an ironic twist, given Isaac's declared attachment to the culinary merits of his son's fare. It is like one of those commercials where the devotees of a particular brand of soft drink are faced with the choice between two unmarked cups and find themselves deceived into declaring a preference for the other variety. Only Isaac's hearing told him the truth, as he discerned that the one speaking to him had the voice of Jacob (Gen.

27:22). But in the face of the evidence of his other senses, he disbelieved his ears.

Jacob played the situation like a consummate professional, proving that he was the smooth brother in every sense of the word. He was not only willing to lie outright to his father, answering his question "Are you really my son, Esau?" with a boldfaced "I am" (Gen. 27:24). He was even willing to invoke God's name in his dissembling, answering Isaac's query as to how he had been able to return so rapidly with this affirmation: "The LORD your God gave me success" (Gen. 27:20). His father was taken in, and Jacob was granted the blessing intended for his brother (Gen. 27:27–29). Isaac invoked upon Jacob the blessing of material fruitfulness and lordship over his brothers, along with the Abrahamic stipulation, "May those who curse you be cursed and those who bless you be blessed."

When Esau returned and discovered the truth of what had happened, he was devastated, but it was too late. The damage had been done, and the blessing could not be retracted (Gen. 27:36–40). There was no second blessing left for Esau. The blessing (*berakah*) had gone the way of the birthright (*bekorah*) he had earlier despised. Seething with rage, Esau planned to murder Jacob after his father died (Gen. 27:41). When Rebekah heard what was going on, she saw that Jacob's only hope was to flee for his life (Gen. 27:44).

PASSING ON THE BLAME

From a human perspective, the whole situation is a mess of cheating and lying. The temptation is to ask "Who's to blame?" and perhaps single out Jacob as primarily responsible, with the aiding and abetting of his mother, Rebekah. Alternatively, because we know that Jacob is ultimately the hero of the narrative, the one through whom the line of promise descends, we might exonerate Jacob for his actions and say that Esau got what was coming to him. After all, he had already despised his birthright twice. Both approaches would be wrong, however. All are to blame; no one emerges from this saga with credit, except for God, whose good purposes endure in spite of the worst efforts of men.

Let's look at the participants one by one.

REBEKAH

It is never wise to stand between a mother and the promotion prospects of her favorite son. If you do, there is a good chance that you will be trampled underfoot. That this motivation is at work in Rebekah's heart is clear from Genesis 27:5–6. She hears Isaac talk to his son (Gen. 27:5) and responds by formulating a plan in favor of her son (Gen. 27:6). The pronouns say it all. Whatever happened to family unity? Somewhere along the way that was lost.

However, although it would be easy to condemn Rebekah as the stereotype of an ambitious Jewish mother, manipulating her husband to get what she wants for her son, that view would be wrong. We also need to see things from her perspective. She had received an oracle from God before the birth of Esau and Jacob, which had declared that the older would serve the younger (Gen. 25:23). That oracle was—from a human perspective—on the point of being frustrated and defeated. It was not that her husband was about to do something unwise or make a decision with which she didn't agree. He was not opting for a couch with stripes when she would have preferred a plain pattern. He was apparently about to thwart the revealed will of God.

God had destined the Abrahamic promise for Jacob's line, and Isaac was about to commit it to the line of Esau.

Isaac lay on what appeared to be his deathbed, and his mind was made up. Once the blessing was delivered, it could not be revoked. Time was short. So what is a believing wife to do? Doesn't the end justify the means? Wouldn't it be better for her to break a few of God's "less important" laws to make sure that his long-term purpose stands?

Do you recognize this temptation? It's one of Satan's favorite shortcuts. He comes to you and suggests that God's promises seem to be taking a long time to work out. Perhaps if we just gave him a little help . . . ? He says to you, "Yes, I know the plan I'm proposing is not exactly kosher in all the details, but how can it be wrong when it will bring about something so good?"

So Satan came to Jesus in the wilderness and showed him all the kingdoms of the world in their splendor, saying, "All this will I give you, if you will bow down and worship me" (Matt. 4:9). He offered Jesus a much simpler way of achieving what he had come to earth to do. What goal could possibly be better? Wouldn't the immediate reign of Jesus over all the kingdoms of earth be a wonderful thing? And this way seemed to avoid the unpleasant necessity of the cross. But Jesus emphatically rejected Satan's shortcut. It is not enough for the goal to be right; the means by which we arrive at that goal must be right also.

As Paul reminds us, for an athlete to win the victor's crown he must not only cross the finish line first; he must also compete according to the rules (2 Tim. 2:5). Our calling is to be obedient to God and let him take care of fulfilling his promises in his way at his time.

The bottom line question that we have to answer is this: Can God fulfill his promises without our help? The issue for Rebekah boils down to the choice between faith and unbelief. When we put it like that, of course, the answer is obvious. There are no "less important" laws in God's Word that can be broken in order to bring about good ends. The solution to one person's sin can never be another sin on our part. God will take care of the ends that he has purposed, according to his promises. Meanwhile, our responsibility is to be faithful in our use of the means he has ordained. Rebekah should have entrusted the issue to God in prayer and watched and waited to see the Lord's hand at work. Nothing is impossible for him.

JACOB

Jacob appears clearly in this story as a cold-blooded, conniving schemer. As we have seen, when he hesitates at first to go along with the plan, it is not because of any moral scruples on his part but because he doubts its practicality (Gen. 27:11). The tempter is easily able to reassure him on that score. He can appear as your fairy godmother, promising to wave his magic wand and enable you to attend the ball of your choice. What he does not reveal to you is that if you give in to him, the gilded carriage of your sin will turn back into its true pumpkin self long before midnight. By the time the cost of your sin becomes clear, there is no longer any way out. Jacob will discover to his cost that he is going to be paying the price of acquiring the blessing in this way for many years to come.

Perhaps one of the most remarkable aspects of fallen humanity is our ability to believe that we can sin and not get hurt. We are so easily convinced by Satan that our sin will not come to light and that if it does it will not hurt us. The Bible, however, warns us against such comfortable illusions when it says, "You may be sure that your sin will find you out" (Num. 32:23). How many people have found that to be true from their bitter experience! Whether it is the preacher who loses his ministry through adultery, or the manager who loses his job through theft, or the man or woman who loses peace through the burden of a secret sin, all sin hurts and costs and destroys. Sooner or later—and usually sooner than we think—sin comes home to roost, often with devastating results. Yet it is remarkable how slow we are to believe that reality. In practice, once you enter a debate with Satan over whether sin is safe, you will always lose. The question But what if I get caught? has no power to send him packing. Even if we do not get caught, the cost of sin is still real.

Once Jacob has been reassured as to the safety of his sin, he goes about it with shocking effectiveness. In Genesis 3, God clothed Adam and Eve in animal skin as a picture of the gospel. In his grace, he demonstrated his willingness to provide an effective covering for the shame that resulted from his creatures' sin. In contrast, Jacob uses animal skin to cover his sinning in a different way. He uses it to enable him to deceive his father about his identity. In the conversation that ensues, he heaps lie upon lie, even invoking the name of the Lord in support of his lies. Has he no shame? Is this the way to achieve God's purposes and secure God's blessing? Surely not.

ISAAC

Then there is Isaac. What shall we say of his part in all of this? What is he doing trying to pass the blessing on to his favorite son, in the light of the clear oracle to the contrary from God? He's no better than Rebekah. At least she could claim the oracle of God in defense of her preference. Isaac had no such excuse. He was seeking to circumvent God's Word in favor of his desires and preferences. Otherwise why was there such a need for stealth on his part? Why was this transaction going to be done in secret, in the bedroom, instead of in front of the whole family? The transfer of the blessing should surely have been part of a devotional service in front of the whole household, not one parent craftily stealing a march on the other! Isaac apparently sought to use God to achieve his desired ends, instead of submitting himself to God's revealed will. Isaac loved his older child for what he could do for his senses, cooking up tasty country food for him to enjoy, and so he sought to pass on the blessing to him. He ended up sadly deceived by the very senses he sought to satisfy.

What a tragic picture: a man at odds with his family, who are all out to get from him whatever they can. Yet Isaac, for all his sinful motivation, is still commended in Hebrews 11:20 specifically for his faith in blessing Jacob. That may seem a strange commendation at first sight. What faith was it when he sought to counteract the revealed will of God and blessed Jacob by accident, as it were? The answer is that although Isaac's faith was mistaken in its direction, it was solid in its heart. Although he was wrong in the one he sought to bless, he was profoundly right in believing that there was a blessing to be transmitted. He believed God that one day the promise delivered through Abraham would bear fruit in the lives of his descendants; it is in those terms that he gives his blessing.

That is no small faith on Isaac's part, especially when you consider how little progress toward that goal had been made in his lifetime. Many years had now passed since the death of Abraham, and Isaac seemed to human eyes almost as far from possessing the blessing in its fullness as his father had been. However, although the visible horizon was empty, Isaac still had his spiritual eyes firmly fixed on the city to come. He believed in the blessing.

Not only that, Isaac was sufficiently a man of faith to recognize his mistake once it was exposed. When Esau came in to him after Jacob had left and the deception became clear, Isaac trembled violently (Gen. 27:33). He trembled because his wrong intentions had been exposed and defeated by God's sovereignty. So when Esau sought a further blessing, Isaac had none to give. He would not try to thwart God a second time. All he could promise Esau was this:

> Your dwelling will be
>   away from earth's richness,
>   away from the dew of heaven above.
> You will live by the sword
>   and you will serve your brother.
> But when you grow restless,
>   you will throw his yoke
>   from off your neck. (Gen. 27:39–40)

This is the negation of all that has been promised to Jacob (see Gen. 27:28–29). Where Jacob had been promised the earth's richest blessing, lordship over other nations, and to be the source of blessing to other people, Esau would have neither prosperity nor lordship nor blessing. What is more, even the blessing that he might have found for himself in Jacob, he will turn his back on. To cast off the yoke of the one chosen by God means choosing the way of curse over the way of blessing. Isaac's recognition of God's choice of Jacob may have come late, but his conversion is sincere. Thus when it comes time for Jacob to leave, he takes with him his father's blessing a second time, this time honestly won (Gen. 28:1–4).

ESAU

It is easy for us to feel sorry for Esau. Is he not the one cheated out of a blessing that ought by rights to have been his? In fact, however, his position is in one sense merely the logical outworking of the earlier deal he made with Jacob. He had sworn by an oath to trade his rights as firstborn to his brother in exchange for a bowl of stew (Gen. 25:29–34). Now that he is trying to get around the consequences of his earlier actions by participating in a subterfuge, there is something fitting in him being deprived of it definitively by means of a bowl of stew. Though he cried over this outcome, there is no evidence that Esau regretted the loss of the birthright and blessing for their spiritual benefits, only for their worldly ones. Never in his whole life does Esau show any sign of seeking after God and remaining separate from the world. His total and continuing lack of any spiritual sensitivity is plain in his choice of wives. First, he married two Hittite women (Gen. 26:34), and then, realizing that his father and mother were not impressed by his discernment, he compounded the mistake by marrying an Ishmaelite (Gen. 28:9).

How many other people, like Esau, lament the mistakes they have made in their earlier lives? They mourn the wasted years, the missed opportunities—but tears are not enough. There must be a genuine heart change. Even yet, Esau could still have found a blessing for himself. It was not to be found in Isaac, from whom he sought it, but rather in Jacob, as he looked in faith to the One who would come, Jacob's greater descendant. "Those who bless you will be blessed" was the enduring promise that God had given to Abraham and his seed (Gen. 12:3; 27:29). Esau should therefore have swallowed his pride and gone to Jacob with tears, seeking forgiveness from him and a share in the blessing as he identified with the promised seed to come through him.

Did he? Not likely. Far from being softened, Esau's heart stored up his anger against Jacob. He planned to kill him (Gen. 27:41). Although Esau's reaction took an extreme form, the basic heart movement is not uncommon. In their later years, many people come to recognize at some level that their lives have been built on the wrong foundation. They discover halfway through that their whole lives have been spent climbing the wrong ladder. However, they will not come to the only One who can bring meaning and hope into their lives, Jacob's greater descendant, Jesus. Instead, their hearts are turned toward anger and bitterness. Esau lamented his folly and the way things had turned out for him, but as far as we can tell, he never repented of his sin in despising his birthright. He had sold his soul to the devil, not for the world but for a bowl of stew. He didn't like the consequences of his actions, but he still would not turn from his sins and come humbly, broken of all self-reliance, giving his hope and trust over to God.

THE CONSEQUENCES OF SIN

Let God be true and every man a liar. Every man and woman in this whole mess has been false to the core. Each of them has been self-seeking, self-trusting, self-serving, using others and trying to use God for their ends. But God's purposes still stand. They may have meant it for evil, but God will use it for good. The well-devised plans of men succeed or are frustrated at God's pleasure, in order to accomplish his goals.

The consequences of taking Satan's shortcut are nonetheless real and often devastating. The clear message of this passage is that sin doesn't pay, even when it gives you what you wanted. This is a lesson we all need to take to heart, for Satan can make his offerings seem so compellingly attractive. He baits his hooks with juicy worms. The real nature of his offerings always comes out in the end, though. In the same way, the sins of all of the participants in this drama will come back to haunt them for the rest of their lives.

The two central protagonists in particular, Rebekah and Jacob, will find their victory bittersweet. Rebekah's plan may win the blessing for her favorite son, but it will also result in his exile from their home forever. Jacob's days of hanging around the tent are over. As far as we know, Rebekah never saw Jacob again after his enforced departure from the family. What is more, Jacob may have been blessed by his father with every material blessing, but he will soon find himself on the road with nothing other than the clothes he stands up in and the rod upon which he leans. It will be a long and hard road before Isaac's words of blessing over Jacob see any fulfillment. Jacob had to learn of his depravity and its consequences not from the pages of a theology textbook but from the bitter fruit of his experience.

THE TRIUMPH OF GRACE

Nonetheless, there is more to it than that. In spite of sin and the bitter fruits that sin brings in its wake, God's purposes to bless his people are eternally secure. Grace is at work in the lives of the patriarchs, and the grace of God will not let them go. In spite of their sin and even through their sin, God can and will achieve what he has planned. He will bring his promised Redeemer, not from picture-perfect parentage but from the offspring of a long line of sinners.

This chapter clearly shows us God's people in need of a redeemer. But it also points us by way of counterexample to what this redeemer would be. Our Redeemer was also to be found dressed in clothes that were not his. But in the case of Jesus, the clothing that he wore at the climactic moment of his life was not the stolen finery of Esau but rather a purple robe on loan from the Roman soldiers and then a shroud borrowed from Joseph of Arimethea. What is more, he took that path not in order to steal someone else's blessing for himself but rather to take upon himself our curse. In the most awesome reversal of all, Jesus would graciously say to us what Rebekah rashly said to her son: "Let the curse fall on me" (Gen. 27:13).

Think about that statement. The words Rebekah said so carelessly, never thinking that they might come true, Jesus also said to us even though he knew the full depths of what he was saying. Jesus took your curse so that you might inherit his blessing. The curse that Jacob deserved for his trickery, the curse that you and I earn for ourselves every day by our manifold sinfulness, was laid upon him, so that the blessing that was rightfully his might be given to us, his undeserving people. Jesus wore the shroud of death that we deserved so that we might lawfully be clothed in our elder brother's garments, the spotless robes of Christ's righteousness.

Ultimately that is why sin is not an option for the believer. How can you continue in sin when that sin was paid for in the torn flesh of Jesus? How can you look longingly upon Satan's offerings when the cross of Christ is in front of your eyes? Christ's love constrains our hearts to seek holiness. The fact that sin has no lasting benefits remains true, but it is not simply because sin doesn't pay that you are to turn your back on the tempter. The fact that sin will not get you what you really want in life is not nearly a powerful enough defense to guard you against the attractiveness of Satan's lies and the fickleness of your heart. Only a deep grasp of the gospel has the power to bring about deep change in your heart. It is knowing the terrible price that has already been paid for your sin that enables you to say no to sin.

A deep grasp of the gospel also means that every time you do sin, every time your depravity is revealed afresh, you will run once again to the cross to seek renewed forgiveness and cleansing. You will seek again the love of Christ stretched out to you, a sinner, in the midst of your sin. You are no longer to ask who's to blame, but instead you are to carry your justly deserved blame to the One who bore it for us. At the cross, there is grace sufficient to cover all of your sin, no matter who you are. Praise God! In Christ, we have received freedom from condemnation and the blessing of peace with God.

FOR FURTHER REFLECTION

1. Why are we always so eager to find someone to blame for everything?
2. In what ways might we be tempted to break God's laws in order to fulfill his purposes?
3. How does sin hurt us?
4. In what ways does grace take even our sin and use it for God's glory and our good?

4

JACOB MEETS HIS MAKER
(GENESIS 28)

It was the dictum of a great American president and consummate politician that "you can fool some of the people all of the time, and all of the people some of the time, but you can't fool all of the people all of the time." Jacob learned that lesson the hard way. He may have tricked Esau and Isaac so that he could steal the birthright—or rather so that he might grasp by human effort what would have been his by divine right. But as a result of his trickery, his life was in danger. He had to flee from his home. His sin had come home to roost.

It is sadly typical of family relationships in that household that his mother, Rebekah, didn't even give the real reason for Jacob's leaving to Isaac. Instead, she pointed to Esau's mixed marriages with Hittite women and said to Isaac, "I'm disgusted with living because of these Hittite women. If Jacob takes a wife from among the women of the land, from Hittite women like these, my life will not be worth living" (Gen. 27:46). Even the reason that she gave for her disgust was pragmatic, based on the fact that Hittite women do not make good daughters-in-law, rather than on the spiritual need for Jacob to marry within the family of promise. It seems that this was a family in which the plain, unvarnished truth was consistently in short supply.

THE SINS OF THE PARENTS

This is a classic case of the sins of the parents being visited one hundred times upon the children. Abraham first set the pattern of deceit in small ways, pretending that Sarah was his sister, not his wife (Gen. 12:13; 20:2). Not only was that pattern of behavior directly imitated by Isaac and Rebekah (Gen. 26:7), but also deceit apparently had become a commonplace of life for them. Jacob was brought up in a world of scheming and conniving parents, with Isaac looking out for Esau and Rebekah looking out for him. So it is little wonder that he grew up understanding how to lie and cheat and deceive. He learned those childhood lessons well. Unlearning them would prove to be far more difficult. It would take long years in the wilderness before Jacob was ready for his place in God's program, and even then the scars of his past would never disappear.

That fact makes me wonder, therefore, what sins we are passing on to our children day by day. We are typically so blind to our shortcomings as parents, until they are reproduced in magnified form in the lives of our children. What are our cherished sins and wrong ways of relating that we will transmit to our offspring? Will they learn from us merely how to abound in sin while successfully concealing it from the sight of others, or will they learn from our constant example how to repent of sin and turn from it? Are you setting an example for your children of godliness and holiness and of rapid and heartfelt repentance when your sin becomes plain, or are you merely modeling for them how to live as an effective sinner? Are there those around you who can freely confront you over areas of your life where you are going astray, or are you defensive and slow to receive criticism?

ISAAC'S BLESSING

Jacob now had to make his own way in the world, leaving the Promised Land in search of a godly wife—or at least one who would not disgust his mother. It was a path that Abraham's servant had trodden before him, successfully seeking a wife for his master's son, Isaac. But Jacob embarked on this long journey with none of the advantages of his predecessor. He traveled alone, on foot, without gifts or resources to promise his future bride. From a human perspective, he seemed unlikely even to reach Laban's house safely, let alone ever to return with a bride. It would turn out to be a much more difficult path for him than it was for Abraham's servant. But at least he went out with Isaac's blessing ringing in his ears:

> May God Almighty bless you and make you fruitful and increase your numbers until you become a community of peoples. May he give you and your descendants the blessing given to Abraham, so that you may take possession of the land where you now live as an alien, the land God gave to Abraham. (Gen. 28:3–4)

This is nothing less than the blessing first given to Abraham, now being legitimately passed on to Jacob (Gen. 28:4). Like that first blessing, this is a blessing that promises multiplied offspring to Jacob (Gen. 28:3). However, it goes further than merely promising Jacob a large quantity of descendants. It also speaks of a particular quality of his descendants.

Jacob's children will not just be many; they will also

become a *community (qahal)* of peoples. What the Hebrew word has in view is not a community of peoples in the sense of an international organization like the United Nations, in which it frequently seems that each nation is continually doing its utmost to protect its interests against those of the rest. Nor will theirs be a brotherhood like that of Isaac and Ishmael or that of Jacob and Esau, with one brother continually in the other brother's face, in an enmity that stretches down across the generations. What God promised to Jacob through Isaac's blessing is nothing less than the beginning of Israel: a true community of brothers dwelling together in unity. In fact, we may even say that this promise is the beginning of the church, since the Septuagint, the Greek translation of the Old Testament, most commonly translates the Hebrew word *qahal* by the Greek word *ekklēsia,* which is the New Testament word for the "church."

As the psalmist says in Psalm 133:1, "How good and pleasant it is when brothers dwell together in unity." Most of us know from experience, in families and in churches, that the unity of which the psalmist speaks is by no means a universal experience in a fallen world. However, it remains God's promise and his goal for his people. Moreover, along with the promise of plentiful descendants came the promise that those united descendants would together inherit the Promised Land (Gen. 28:4). Though Jacob must now leave the land of Canaan, he was not to forget that the land belonged to him and to his children by rights.

As for Esau, when he heard of Jacob's departure in search of a spiritually suitable wife, he seemed to be convicted of his sin in marrying into the pagan families that filled the land. But even then, he didn't seem to know how to make it better. In fact, Esau compounded his earlier sin by marrying an Ishmaelite girl to add to his Hittite wives. Isn't this a vivid picture of the way of the heart without God? Even when such persons try to do the things that are moral and upright, they increase their sin, because they don't understand the nature of God or the depth of their natural depravity. As Paul puts it in Romans 1, their minds are darkened and cannot perceive God's truth. They are blind to spiritual realities, a blindness that only God can remove.

JACOB AT BETHEL

Meanwhile, the sun was setting on Jacob, and he found a place to stop for the night (Gen. 28:11). The setting of the sun is not merely an incidental detail in the story. This detail vividly depicts Jacob's situation: night had caught up with him. The sun would not rise for him, from the perspective of the narrative, until Genesis 32. At that time, on his return from exile, he would have another dramatic encounter with God, only this time while the sun was coming up at the fords of the Jabbok. In the meantime, he would have to endure the long, dark night of exile from the land.

Nonetheless these two encounters with God, which bracket his time away from the Promised Land, graciously demonstrated God's enduring presence with him in the long night in between. What an encouragement this is to those who have spent years wandering in the wilderness. Even Jacob's sins could not separate him from the loving presence of God, nor could they prevent him ultimately from inheriting what God had promised. The grace of God would ultimately triumph in his life. Though his sins had serious and lasting consequences, the promise would ultimately be fulfilled because of God's faithfulness, in spite of Jacob's unfaithfulness.

As it turned out, the place where he had chosen to camp was no ordinary place. It was a *maqom*. Now *maqom* is a Hebrew word with a double meaning. It can mean "place," as it appears in the English translations.

However, the word can also be used to refer to an especially sacred place. The place where Jacob stopped for the night was truly a *maqom* in the latter sense. Although Jacob thought that it was an ordinary place, an unplanned stopover on his weary road to an apparently dark future, he was soon to find out otherwise. The place where he was sleeping would turn out to be none other than *beth-el*, the "house of God." There at Bethel, as we would call it, God revealed himself to Jacob in a dream. It was not a vision of a ladder, as it is traditionally described, but rather of a stone staircase going up from earth to heaven filled with angelic traffic between God and man (Gen. 28:12).

BETHEL AND BABEL

The background for this vision is the Tower of Babel story. That tower was a ziggurat, a stepped-pyramid temple, which was conceived as essentially a similar kind of stone stairway to the heavens (Gen. 11:4). The builders of Babel had a dual purpose for their building program. By building the tower, they sought to find for themselves security ("so that we . . . may not be scattered") and significance ("that we may make a name for ourselves"). Neither of these goals was achieved. They were scattered by the decisive judgment of God, and the name they made for themselves was as a proverbial failure. Instead of making the Gate of God (the original meaning of the word *Babel*), what they built was the archetypal house of confusion. Jacob's encounter with God, in stark contrast to that of the builders of Babel, was unsought for, unexpected, and undeserved. He had done nothing in his life to earn God's favor; quite the reverse, he was a liar and a cheat. All he was looking for was a place to lay his head and rest on his journey.

Yet he found something far greater. What the builders

of Babel sought in vain was graciously given to unde-serving Jacob: the promise of security (Gen. 28:15) and significance (Gen. 28:14). God appeared to him and said:

> I am the LORD, the God of your father Abraham and the God of Isaac. I will give you and your de-scendants the land on which you are lying. Your descendants will be like the dust of the earth, and you will spread out to the west and to the east, to the north and to the south. All peoples on earth will be blessed through you and your offspring. I am with you and will watch over you wherever you go, and I will bring you back to this land. I will not leave you until I have done what I have promised you. (Gen. 28:13–15)

What God promised Jacob was nothing short of the covenant made with Abraham. Just as his father had sought in his blessing, so the Lord confirmed the Abra-hamic blessing to Jacob. Ironically this happened at the moment at which it must have seemed to Jacob that all was lost, when it was evident that all his scheming had misfired. He was on the run with no prospect of inherit-ing the promise, humanly speaking. But this irony is nec-essary. God came to Jacob at his lowest point in order that it may be seen clearly that all is of grace, unmerited, undeserved favor. Indeed, it is a double misnomer to call the stairway to heaven Jacob's ladder, for Jacob had no part in building it or traversing it. Rather, it was God's stairway, whereby he reaffirmed the constancy of his lov-ing care for his chosen but rebellious child.

GOD'S ANSWER TO BABEL

Some of you can probably relate to Jacob's experi-ence. You too sought security and significance in all the wrong places. God came to you not when you were on top of the world but when your world had caved in upon you. God took you through dark times in order to reveal his light to you. God sought you when you were not seeking him, and in spite of the fact that there was nothing good in you to draw him. God in his grace sought you out and revealed himself to you. Perhaps some of you are at Bethel now, waiting to be surprised by the grace of God.

But Jacob's experience was even more profound than ours. For what God was doing at Bethel is nothing less than reversing the earlier judgment upon humankind at the tower of Babel (Gen. 11). This place, Bethel, is the true gate of heaven, not Babel (Gen. 28:17). Here it becomes clear that God will reveal himself to men, on his timetable, through his chosen line. What humankind could never do for themselves, even by working together in perfect harmony, will begin to be brought about by God in the life of undeserving Jacob. Even a perfect United Nations could never bring about true and lasting peace for humanity. But there is an answer to our need for peace and unity. God's answer to the tragic dividedness of the post-Babel world is the community of peoples that he will establish through Jacob, the forefather of Israel.

The reality to which this dream points was only partially realized in the history of Old Testament Israel. They frequently failed to live up to the dream of a united people of God. The nation of Israel was divided in the time of Rehoboam, Solomon's son, into two separate and frequently hostile realms. However, the vision of a single, united people of God worshiping the Lord together remained alive into the exile and beyond (see Ezek. 37:15–28). The prophets still anticipated the day when the brotherhood of unity among Israel's warring tribes would be realized.

The fulfillment of the promise was not realized until the coming of Jesus. Thus, addressing the prospective disciple Nathanael, whom he describes as "a true Israelite, in whom there is nothing false" (i.e., someone not like the original Israel, Jacob), Jesus told him that he would see heaven opened and angels ascending and descending upon the Son of man (John 1:51). The reference to Jacob's dream at Bethel is clear. Jesus is the true stairway to heaven, the only way to God. His coming is the only means by which fellowship and friendship between God and man can be reestablished. In him alone, we find true security and true significance for our lives. It is through his death and resurrection alone that grace comes to filthy, rotten scoundrels like Jacob, and like you and me, so that we can be called the people of God.

This new relationship with God spills over into our relationship with other people as well. We go from being mere fellow travelers through life to forming part of a new community. This was what Jesus prayed for in his high-priestly prayer in John 17: that his followers would be one even as he and the Father are one—a single people of God, bound together in an intimate spiritual unity. What is more, in Jesus the boundaries of the community of peoples, the true Israel of God, extend more broadly than the physical descendants of Jacob to take in all who by faith are the spiritual descendants of Abraham. By faith in Christ, the Gentiles too are incorporated into the one new people of God.

JACOB'S RESPONSE

What was Jacob's response to the God who revealed himself to him? In the first place, he was surprised. You might say, "Of course he was surprised! God had just appeared to him in a dream," yet elsewhere in Genesis the rest of the patriarchs seem to take such revelations in stride. Jacob alone was astonished by God's self-revelation, perhaps because he realized how little he deserved it. After he recovered from his surprise and initial fear, however, he went on to respond with total self-commitment. His vow in Genesis 28:20 echoed exactly God's promise to him in Genesis 28:15. If God would undertake to be his God, just as he was the God of his forefathers, Abraham and Isaac, then he in return would give himself completely to God. If the Lord would be with him and provide for him bread and clothes, the basic necessities of life, then he in turn would worship this God, a vow sealed by his commitment of a tithe (one-tenth) of all that the Lord would bless him with.

So also you and I must respond to the God who has revealed himself to us in Jesus. It is not enough to be surprised and impressed by what the Bible says about God. It is not enough to find the company of Christians appealing and attractive. God demands of those who would be his people nothing less than total self-commitment. For Jacob, tangible expression of that self-commitment took the form of a voluntary vow to tithe. Living as he did before the giving of the law through Moses at Sinai, he was not bound by the obligation to give an annual tithe of the fruits of the soil in the way his descendants were. But the effect of the grace he had received was to create a heart that wanted to give something back to God. This was not natural for Jacob. By nature, he was a go-getter, someone who thought that it is more blessed to get than to give. His ambition was to be a self-made man, beholden to no one. But now he was being transformed by grace from a go-getter into a go-giver.

Has grace had that impact upon your life also? We, like the patriarchs, are not bound by the requirement in the law of Moses to give an annual tithe. That was part of Israel's civil law, which bound them as long as they lived in the land to give one-tenth of their agricultural produce to the Lord, as a mark of the Lord's ownership of the land. As a matter of fact, because the tithe required under the Mosaic order was specifically a tithe of agricultural produce (see Lev. 27:30; Deut. 14:22–23), it wouldn't be hard for someone like me to tithe. I'd bring along an orange and a couple of grapefruit to church once a year, and I'd be home free. But shall I give less because I am under grace than I would have been obligated to give under law? By no means! If my heart has been touched by grace, then no one should have to pester me to tithe. My giving should not be driven by a sense of guilt but by an overwhelming and awed sense of gratitude for the gospel. I should be eager to be "a cheerful giver" (2 Cor. 9:7), someone who because of the grace I have received delights to excel in what Paul calls "the grace of giving" (2 Cor. 8:7).

In token of his commitment to the Lord, Jacob raised up a *matsevah*, a standing stone. This stone was more than a mere witness to God's act of self-revelation. In a significant way, the standing stone depicts the dream. Like the stone, the staircase in the dream was itself "set up" (*mutsav*), while at its top the Lord was "standing" (*nitsav;* a related Hebrew word). The top (*rosh*) of the staircase was in the heavens, while it is the top (*rosh*) of the standing stone that Jacob anoints with oil, symbolizing the source of his blessing. As we shall see, stones became something of a theme in the life of Jacob, and this one was to be a perpetual reminder of his encounter with the grace of God. To this miniature depiction of the vision, Jacob would return to worship God (Gen. 35) when the promises made in the vision were fulfilled.

Jacob's response to God's gracious self-revelation was thus not simply to commit himself to give; he also committed himself to worship. This is as it should be. If the entries in your checkbook are one key indicator of the vitality of your spiritual life, your hunger for worship is another. Like our giving, our regular attendance at church should not be a guilt-driven obligation but rather an expression of awed gratitude for God's love revealed to us in Jesus Christ. A Christian without a deep desire to worship is a contradiction in terms. It is like a sports fan who never wishes to attend a single game of his favorite team or a music buff who never wants to go to a concert.

If Jacob was moved to worship by his experience of God, how much more should we be moved to worship as Christians, for we come to God through the gate of heaven to which Bethel pointed forward, Jesus. Jacob was drawn to worship by the privilege of standing at the bottom of the staircase that led to God; that was evidence to him of God's amazing grace. In Christ, however, we do not merely stand at the bottom of the stairway, gazing up. In Christ, we are able to ascend the heavenly Mount Zion, to approach and enter the throne room of God, there to bow down before him and to worship him acceptably with reverence and awe (Heb. 12:22–29). In view of that privilege, how can our hearts be so slow to worship?

RETURNING TO BETHEL

There are, however, two other points we need to notice about Jacob's experience of God at Bethel. We see that Jacob was not instantaneously transformed into a holy person by his encounter with God. In spite of God's promise of protection, when trouble seems to be looming, he will continue to try to scheme his way out of it. Old habits die hard. The road to sanctification for Jacob was long and gradual and ultimately incomplete in this life.

So it is also with us. We are faced daily with the choice between trusting the promise or falling into habitual patterns of sin. How frequently in our experience sin wins out over faith in the promise! Doubtless, during those times in his life, Jacob would have had to return frequently to Bethel in his mind and recall the reality of God's grace. So also we should frequently remind ourselves of the grace of God shown to us in the cross of Christ, especially when we have sinned. This is a spiritual journey upon which we have been given the Lord's Supper as a vital help. As Paul tells us, "Whenever you eat this bread and drink this cup, you proclaim the Lord's death" (1 Cor. 11:26). We proclaim the death of Christ not simply as the general answer to the sins of the world but also to ourselves as the particular answer to our sin. Our hunger to be reminded of grace should make us long to come to the Lord's table often and should make our experience of God's grace there deep and precious.

Notice, however, that Bethel would later become a snare to Israel. In Amos 5:5, judgment is pronounced on the sanctuary that subsequently developed at Bethel. Through the prophet, the Lord says,

> Seek me and live;
>> do not seek Bethel,
> do not go to Gilgal,
>> do not journey to Beersheba.
> For Gilgal will surely go into exile,
>> and Bethel will be reduced to nothing.

The problem was that the place where God once met with his people had become an alternative to meeting the living God. The house of God had been turned into a house of idolatry. A similar shift happened with the bronze snake that Moses lifted up in the wilderness. What had once been a means of deliverance to the people from a plague of deadly snakes (Num. 21:9) later became an object of idolatry among the people (2 Kings 18:4).

This is a repeated problem in the lives of God's people. Traditions, ancient and modern, can so easily replace reality in our worship. Can we identify the idols that we tend to cherish in our hearts, the traditions that have become more important than encounter with the living God? What for us are the places where God met with his people in the past but does so no more? Perhaps for some of us the Reformation has become more important than the Bible and the question of what Calvin would do more interesting than what the Bible tells us to do. Catechisms and confessions are likewise a great blessing, but in some churches they can almost come to take the place of the Scriptures as our primary reference points of orthodoxy. By contrast, some people are so attached to certain forms of worship or certain styles of music (new or old) that they feel that they can't possibly worship God without them. As we consider these possibilities, it is probably easy for us to identify and condemn the sins of others in this area, but do we see as clearly our idolatries? How easily good things, things that were intended for our blessing, can become snares to each of us!

If Abraham is the archetypal man of faith, Jacob is surely the archetypal picture of grace. The schemer whose wonderful schemes have backfired is now a fugitive on the run for his life, stranded in the dark in the wilderness. Yet this is the one to whom God chooses to reveal himself, and his grace will not be without effect in Jacob's life. The promised blessings that Jacob sought to wangle for himself will ultimately be given to him. But they will not come through might or through power or even through his craftiness but through the spirit of God.

Ultimately grace comes to Jacob just as it comes to us, through the death of the Son of God, who came to restore community between God and humanity, Jesus. He is the One who is the way, the truth, and the life. He is the real stairway to heaven. He is the One through whom we must come if we are to come to God. In him alone are to be found security and significance, blessing for ourselves and for others. Indeed, every spiritual blessing is ours in him (Eph. 1). These are blessings you cannot trick your way into, as Jacob tried to do; they are blessings you cannot organize for yourself, as the builders of Babel sought to do; rather, they are blessings that have been freely given by God to all whom he has chosen and called and whom he brings into relationship with him. Praise be to God for his wonderful grace to us!

FOR FURTHER REFLECTION

1. What sins have you learned from your family? How can we set good patterns for our children to follow?
2. What is God's answer to Babel?
3. How does God's answer to Babel meet our need for a way back to God? How does it address the real problems that face our world?
4. How are you and I called to respond to Bethel?
5. What dangers does the subsequent history of Bethel make clear to us? How might those dangers be present in your church and in your heart?

5

THE WILDERNESS YEARS

(GENESIS 29:1-30)

Great leaders often spend long years in which their gifts are either unused or, as yet, unusable before their rise to greatness. Winston Churchill is a classic example. At a young age, he caught the attention of Britain during the Boer War in South Africa, when he played a key part in foiling a Boer assault on an armored train. Although he was captured, he promptly escaped in dramatic fashion. After his return home, Churchill became a prominent politician during the early part of the First World War. Later, however, he fell out of favor. He was regarded as something of a loose cannon, unreliable in his judgment, and he spent most of the years between the First and Second World Wars on the fringes of power. No one trusted him enough to give him a major responsibility in leadership.

Churchill did not return to the center of the action until the outbreak of the Second World War confirmed the accuracy of his prophetic warnings about the danger posed by Nazi Germany. On the day war broke out, he was installed as First Lord of the Admiralty, in charge of the navy. Within a year, he replaced Neville Chamberlain as Prime Minister after the fall of France to the Germans. At that point, it became clear to all that he was the only figure who could command the support of all of the various political factions. The rest, as they say, is history: Churchill was at center stage for what was his, and perhaps also Britain's, finest hour.

TRAINING FOR GREATNESS

A similar pattern of training for greatness is common in the Bible. A place of leadership over God's people frequently follows a period of lengthy preparation in the wilderness of exile, far from the limelight. This common pattern links Abraham, whose call to service came at age seventy-five, and Moses, who kept his father-in-law's sheep before being turned loose on God's flock, and David, who spent years on the run as an outcast before rising to the throne God had promised him. For each, God's way to glory passed through the valley of humiliation.

In contrast, lesser figures in God's program require less preparation. Is this perhaps why Isaac, who is the least prominent of the patriarchs in Genesis, led a relatively smooth life? There was no real conflict over the birthright in his case, even though he too was the younger son. His wife was delivered to him on a silver platter, as it were, through the faithful ministrations of Abraham's servant. I wonder, did Isaac need less preparation because he was a less significant player in God's game plan? His most important acts were to be born and (almost) to be offered up as a living sacrifice. In those key events, he was a passive rather than active participant.

The same could not be said of Jacob. His life was marked by conflict and strife from before day one. Even in the womb, life was a struggle for Jacob. In Genesis 29 he found himself thrust out into the world as a fugitive, little prepared to live by faith. He had been reared in a world of plotting and conniving, of parents who tipped the scales of justice in the direction of their favorite child.

He had learned how to lie and scheme well enough. He thought himself well-equipped to play the world's games in the world's ways.

However, the world that Jacob was entering would test his abilities in this department. His uncle Laban was a picture of worldly shrewdness and unscrupulousness, his match in every way. There's a lesson here for us. Sometimes we're tempted to abandon the way of faith because it seems unlikely to work. It appears to us that honesty is not the best policy. So we turn instead to human strategy and manipulation. But if you take on the world at its own game, you'll almost invariably be outdone. There are plenty of Uncle Labans out there.

What is more, even if you do prevail through your ingenious schemes, as Jacob does in the end, the result is never *shalom*, harmony and peace in all your relationships, but bitter strife, enmity, and soured relationships with those around you. How many people have sought to win the world, in the world's way, and have won—yet have paid a high price in broken and soured relationships with those closest to them? Honesty may not always be the best policy, as a policy, but dishonesty is always a miserable policy, even when it succeeds.

THE WOMAN AT THE WELL

All this was still in the future for Jacob when he set out from Bethel. He embarked on his journey with renewed energy—the Hebrew literally says "he picked up his feet and went" (Gen. 29:1)—revitalized by his vision of God and with God's blessing upon him ringing in his ears. The evidence of God's continued presence with him seemed clear when he arrived in Paddan Aram and happened upon a well in a field surrounded by shepherds and their flocks. These shepherds told Jacob that they knew Laban. What is more, they confirmed that Laban's present state was *shalom,* peace (Gen. 29:6). That state of affairs would not last long with Jacob around.

This scene at the well must have reminded Jacob of the family stories his mother had told him of her first meeting with Abraham's servant at a similar well (Gen. 24). The similarity was reinforced by the prompt arrival of Laban's gorgeous daughter Rachel and her sheep (Gen. 29:6). Jacob was so moved by the sight of Rachel and the sheep that he performed a feat of extraordinary strength, single-handedly moving the large stone that the combined shepherds of three flocks had claimed to be unable to move (Gen. 29:8, 10). He then watered Laban's sheep and kissed Rachel (Gen. 29:11). These may seem to us utterly unrelated actions, but their parallel nature is clear in the Hebrew, in which the words "he watered" and "he kissed" contain the same consonants. One might almost say that his mouth watered equally at the sight of Laban's daughter and of his flocks. The focus of the next few chapters will be to show how Jacob succeeded in stealing both away from Laban.

For now, however, the focus is on Jacob's exhibition of his competence as a shepherd. Although in comparison with Esau he may have been a homebody, preferring the tents to the open fields (Gen. 25:27), he was no wimp. He also knew that good shepherds should be out with their flocks in the fields at that time of day, unlike the work-shy hirelings around the well. He may even have perceived a possible job opening in Laban's household in that area. Rachel is described as a "shepherdess" (Gen. 29:9), the only woman to hold that job title in Scripture. Shepherding was a tough job in those days, as Jacob notes in Genesis 31:38–40, and therefore it was normally seen as a male role. Rachel is unlikely to have been averse to the prospect of someone else to take her place in the fields.

We shouldn't miss, however, the contrast between our first glimpse of Rachel and our earlier first glimpse of Rebekah. Both had similar encounters at the well that led to their marriages, and both were apparently outstandingly beautiful (Gen. 24:16; 29:17). However, Abraham's servant was not convinced of divine guidance by means of Rebekah's good looks. Even after he saw that she was beautiful, he waited to see if she would fulfill the test of character he had laid out before the Lord. He waited until she proved by her willing and eager service in watering his camels that she was the one the Lord had chosen for his master's son (Gen. 24:21). Moreover, everything Abraham's servant did, from start to finish, was bathed in prayer and conducted in the name of the Lord.

In contrast, while Jacob may have adequately demonstrated his physical strength to Rachel, he knew next to nothing about her apart from her good looks before he decided that she was the one for him. Looks alone are a dangerously deceptive basis on which to choose a bride (Prov. 31:30). He was the one who watered her animals, not vice versa. There was no word of prayer on his lips for divine guidance or any indication that such guidance was what he sought. Rachel was his choice, and he intended to earn her fairly and squarely by his works, not by grace.

JACOB AND LABAN

The same contrast persists in the conversations of the two men with Laban. In Genesis 24, Abraham's servant repeatedly invoked the name of the Lord, praising God for leading him to his master's relatives, asserting that his master's wealth is a gift from God and claiming that the Lord's guidance had led him to Laban and Rebekah. Abraham's servant was the kind of man who makes everyone around him think in God-centered categories. Having heard the whole story, Bethuel and Laban had little choice but to say in response, "This is from the LORD; we can say nothing to you one way or the other. Here is Rebekah; take her and go, and let her become the wife of your master's son, as the LORD has directed" (Gen. 24:50–51).

In contrast, in the same situation Jacob told Laban "all these things" (Gen. 29:13). All what things? we wonder. The text is deliberately enigmatic. Presumably he didn't tell Laban about his deceit in stealing the birthright and blessing—although if he had, there would have been an ironic appropriateness to Laban's saying to him, "You are my own flesh and blood" (Gen. 29:14). He was indeed sprung from the same mold as Laban! However, the name of the Lord is as conspicuously absent from Jacob's lips as it was conspicuously present on the lips of Abraham's servant. The result was that Laban didn't feel it necessary to talk about the Lord either. In contrast to the sending-off of Rebekah, which was an act of faith in the God who controls all things, the agreement between Jacob and Laban was a straight business deal. Laban asked Jacob to name his wages, and he did: one daughter = seven years' hard labor.

Perhaps in his impoverished state Jacob didn't feel that he could make a credible claim to God's blessing. Yet that was what God had promised him (Gen. 28:13–15). On the basis of his father's blessing and the blessing of God at Bethel, he could by faith have revealed himself to Laban as the bearer of the Abrahamic promise. He could have asked for Rachel to be given to him so that together they might return to the Promised Land to build a family for God's glory there. If he had approached the situation on the basis of who he was by grace through faith, how much of the subsequent conflict and sin might have been avoided? But instead of living his life in the light of Bethel, Jacob accommodated himself to the world's way of doing things—and ultimately he paid the price for that decision.

How often do you and I do the same? We have a heavenly Father, from whom nothing in all creation can separate us, yet we live in practice as though we were orphans, reliant on our strength for every good thing that we have. We are united to Christ, our elder brother, who daily intercedes for us at the throne of grace, yet the least problem in our lives causes us to feel abandoned by God and unloved, thrown back on our ingenuity and resources. We have been given the gift of the Holy Spirit to empower our praying, even when we do not know how to pray, yet we frequently give up on prayer because it seems to us as if nothing much is happening. We do not live as what we are: children of the King and heirs of the kingdom!

Think about your circumstances. What issues are causing you to despair because you don't have the ability to resolve them? Are there any situations in your life that you have committed to God recently, knowing that you cannot possibly be the answer to your prayers? How often have you prayed, "Lord, if you are not on our side, the floodwaters of life will sweep me away" (see Ps. 124)? Or do you have a plan of campaign that covers every emergency, an implicit faith that providing you accomplish everything on your to-do list, then God will virtually be able to take the day off? That is my temptation.

This despairing self-dependence may show up in many different areas. In your devotional life, your focus may be on your efforts to get through to God, to put together the right schedule of Bible readings or the right form of words when you pray, rather than on pleading with God to speak to you through his Word and to warm your naturally ice-cold heart. In dealing with your children, you may have read all the books and have developed a ten-point plan for rearing the perfect Christian family instead of recognizing that even your best efforts, without God's intervention, will produce well-washed Pharisees. In your church, the focus may easily become the need to get the right pastor and the right five-year development plan rather than recognizing that without God's work in your midst, your church will be as worthless as a one-legged stool.

There is nothing wrong with planning, studying the issues, and working hard, but unless God is pleased to glorify himself in and through us, all of our many labors will be in vain and the pressures of trying to organize our lives will crush us. We too often need to refresh our memories with the good news that Jacob heard at Bethel: God is with us and has promised never to leave us or forsake us.

IN THE MORNING, LEAH!

This temptation to put our stock in the world's ways of working is particularly strong when we find ourselves in the wilderness. No matter how recently we have come from Bethel and have heard God reiterate his personal care for us, when we find ourselves again in the midst of the reality gap, the gap between what we see and what God has promised, the old temptations come at us again. The repeated temptation in those situations is to compromise, to seek to solve the problems of the world by the ways of the world. That temptation must be resisted, however, not least because it doesn't bridge the gap. As Jacob discovered, making an agreement to operate according to the world's ways often leaves you short of fulfillment and disappointed. You wake up in the morning and there in the bed next to you is Leah, not the Rachel you thought you were getting!

In arranging his deal with Laban, Jacob thought that he had been careful in specifying which daughter he wanted as his wages. He sought the younger, beautiful one, Rachel, not the one with doubtful eyesight, Leah (Gen. 29:18). But with Laban, what you see is not necessarily what you get. Jacob does not serve Laban for nothing, but what he gets from Laban serves him right. For Laban's deception of Jacob is a case of the punishment fitting the crime. The words that Jacob says to Laban—"Why have you deceived me?" (Gen. 29:25)—could just as well have been directed to him by his own father. The answer of Laban, "It is not our custom here to give the younger daughter in marriage before the older one," is likewise an implicit rebuke. In his place, Jacob may have supplanted his elder brother, but he is no longer in his place. He is a stranger now.

Even the manner of the deception echoes Jacob's tricks. Jacob was first wined and dined by Laban and then deceived in the dark, just as he had first fed his father, Isaac, and then taken advantage of the old man's blindness. As it turned out, it was not the weakness of Leah's eyes that was the problem but rather the inability of Jacob's eyes to discern who was in the tent with him that caused his mistake. At the crucial moment, he was just as blind as Isaac had been. In the morning, when it was too late, it all became painfully clear. There in the bed beside him was Leah. In order to acquire Rachel, he would have to serve Laban for another seven years, although this time at least he received payment up front.

PAINFUL PROVIDENCE

Should we feel sympathy for Jacob? Perhaps we should not feel too sorry for him. Even though from his perspective events turned out in a way that was unjust and unfair, this too was part of God's good providence for him. This too is part of the "love that wilt not let me go," as the hymn writer termed it. Of course, it is sometimes not immediately clear that it is good news that

God will not let us go! The marble can hardly expect to enjoy the attentions of the sculptor as piece after piece gets chipped away. Sometimes, perhaps, Jacob wished God would let him be like other men. But God's grace had laid hold of him and would not give him up. The rough, chiseling work of sanctification was in progress in Jacob's life.

At times it must have seemed to Jacob as if his life circumstances were an *anti*-fulfillment of Isaac's blessing that "you shall be a community of peoples" (Gen. 28:3). God, you cannot be serious! *This* Jacob is the one who is going to inherit the Promised Land and through whose multitude of harmonious descendants the world will be blessed? By the end of Genesis 29, he had worked his heart out for his uncle for fourteen years, and all he had earned were two wives who couldn't get along with each other or even (as we shall see in the next chapter) with him. But grace is more powerful than we ever dreamed. Though when you're in the reality gap you may not be able to see how it will ever happen, God's promises stand secure and will prevail. God's purpose for good in sanctifying you in and through trials and suffering may not be comfortable, but it is sure. Even rough diamonds like Jacob—and like you and me—will be polished by providence until we shine like stars.

THE HOPE OF THE WORLD

How can this be? How can God love so much a man like Jacob, who has not set his house or his heart in order? It turns our categories upside down. We think that God ought to help those who help themselves and to reveal himself to decent, moral, God-fearing folk, not to liars and cheats. Were there no upstanding citizens at this time, that God had to resort to dealing with a man like this, a man who had not learned to trust God and tell the truth? But that is how God works. By grace, he chooses the unworthy and the unwashed, and having chosen him, the grace of God will not let him go.

What is God's plan in choosing people like this? Strangely enough, the answer is clarified through another encounter between a man and a woman at a well, many centuries later. There in Samaria, at a well dug by Jacob, Jesus met a woman whose lifestyle made even Jacob seem like an upstanding citizen (John 4:4–26). Once again, it was not to the righteous that God revealed himself but to a notorious sinner, a woman who had scandalized the neighborhood with a Hollywood-style series of marriages and divorces. Not that she was particularly eager to flaunt her dubious lifestyle before a stranger. She answered Jesus' question about her husband evasively. But he apparently knew all about her history and her present behavior. Nor would Jesus be diverted onto safe topics of conversation, such as perennial theological controversies over worship. Rather, he told her that he had come to offer her living water, a gift that would well up into eternal life in her soul (John 4:13). He had come, he said, because the Father is continually seeking worshipers, worshipers who would bow before him in spirit and in truth.

The worshipers God seeks are not those whose lives are together but those who will become the showcases of his grace. He provides all the goodness they will ever need in Jesus Christ; all they contribute is their emptiness and need. The result of Jesus' conversation with the woman at the well was life for her and many of her townspeople. The Father was finding and welcoming in the worshipers he sought.

The hope of the world is not Jacob. He can water Rachel's flock, but he can't water her thirsty soul. Jacob can't change her heart, or even his, so that rivers of living water will flow out from it. On the contrary, from Jacob flow out spreading circles of deceit and confusion.

But God is not finished with Jacob. He will take this schemer and transform him through rough providences, until he is a showcase of God's grace. He too will return to worship the God of Bethel, the God of all grace, and will eventually abandon all of his clever strategies.

What about you? Are you a showcase of God's grace? Do you know the depth of the sin and depravity that remains in your heart? Do you know yourself to be by nature an unlikely candidate for God's love and goodness? Have you experienced God's relentless pursuit of you, so that you too will be a worshiper? Then praise God, who will not let you go now but through whatever rough providences it takes will slowly shape you into the person he wants you to become. Take comfort from the good news that though God starts with the most flawed of material, he will not stop until he has transformed your soul into an object of eternally breathtaking beauty.

God takes only bent instruments and slowly begins to straighten them. He takes only untuned hearts and slowly begins to tune them to his praise. It all takes time, but God is not in a hurry. God's consistent purpose, during whatever times of exile and disappointment he takes you through, is to prepare you for future service and a deepened appreciation of his grace (Eph. 2:10). Submit to his loving purpose, therefore, willingly and ungrudgingly. The wilderness years are indeed hard. Ask Jacob! But the wilderness is not our home. Laban's house is not Jacob's place, as he reminds Jacob. Laban's house is his temporary address. Jacob's place is at Bethel, the place where God first revealed himself to Jacob by his grace. Home, for Jacob and for you and me, is on the other side of the wilderness, where we shall be in God's house forever, tuned with perfect pitch. In the meantime, we listen intently for the sounds of home, and the faint strains of that foreign song summon us on through the weary desert. The reminders of God's grace fill us with renewed vigor and grateful, thankful, longing hearts.

FOR FURTHER REFLECTION

1. How is God preparing Jacob for his kingdom through his encounters with Laban?
2. In what ways does Jacob's encounter at the well expose his heart?
3. In what ways do you demonstrate in your life that you think of yourself as an orphan, left to your resources? When is that temptation strongest in your life?
4. How has God answered your orphan state? What difference should that make in your life this week?

6

THE ARMS RACE

(GENESIS 29:31–30:24)

What's in a name? Faced with this portion of the Genesis story, we may be tempted to cry out, like Shakespeare's Juliet, "Wherefore art thou, Reuben . . . and Simeon . . . and Levi . . . and Judah . . . and what difference does it make anyway?" What spiritual value could there possibly be in a narrative consisting largely of births and names?

Part of our problem, perhaps, is that in our culture we have moved away from the practice of giving our children names that mean something. We no longer name our children after the virtues we hope that they will embody or after Bible characters, as our Puritan ancestors would have done. Nowadays, parents often give their children a name because they like the way it sounds or because it is the name of their favorite movie star or singer. Perhaps our children are glad not to have to go to elementary school burdened with a name like Patience or Mercy or Increase or Ichabod. The result, though, is that our little Kyle or Britney could just as easily have been called Brandon or Vicky without it changing our view of them. What indeed is in a name?

In the Book of Genesis, however, names have meanings. In some cases, the meaning would be transparently obvious to a native speaker of Hebrew, as in the name Ishmael, which comes from the phrase "God [*El*] hears [*shama'*]." In others, the naming is based on a pun or wordplay, as in the name Adam (*adam*), which sounds like the word for "ground" (*adamah*). Either way, there was often a connection between the circumstances of the birth and the name given to the child. Because of this feature of the Genesis narrative, the list of the names given to Jacob's twelve sons by Leah and Rachel opens a window into their thinking. The children's names are a reflection of the life-or-death power struggle in which the two wives of Jacob were locked—a conflict for the attentions and affections of their shared husband. Whoever won this arms race and secured his embraces stood to gain security and prestige for herself as the bearer of his sons. The loser, in a society where a woman's value was normally measured by the number of her sons, was doomed to a seemingly worthless existence on the sidelines of life.

This ancient fact of life was all the more pronounced in the case of Rachel and Leah, for their spouse was no ordinary family man. Jacob was the bearer of the Abrahamic blessing (Gen. 28:4) and along with it the ancient promise of a future seed who would crush the serpent's head (Gen. 3:15). Which of the two dueling sisters would be the mother of the Messiah? Would the blessing pass once again through the line of the younger, with the older sibling left out in the cold, as with Jacob and Esau? Or would God this time favor the older one, Leah, because she was unloved and disadvantaged? There was much at stake in this conflict, though the pair actively involved seem no more motivated by spiritual concerns than Esau and Jacob were before them in their struggle over the birthright.

GOD'S LOVE TO THE UNLOVED

As our passage opens, God's favor is shown first to the unlovely and unloved, Leah, so that she was the first to bear a son (Gen. 29:31). The term "not loved" or "despised" is not merely an emotional description of Jacob's relationship with Leah. The Hebrew word also has technical, legal connotations that highlight the insecurity of Leah's position in Jacob's household. Leah was the unfavored wife, who in that culture would be in constant danger of being cast off, mistreated, or divorced. Such a status was not surprising given the fact that Jacob didn't have any intention of marrying her to begin with. She was, if not the ugly sister, at least the less attractive one, who was foisted on Jacob through her father's trickery. When Jacob expected to find Rachel in bed with him the morning after his wedding, there was Leah instead (Gen. 29:25). This was hardly an auspicious start for any marriage.

Leah's precarious position was then compounded by Laban's giving of Rachel to Jacob as well, as advance payment for another seven years of work (Gen. 29:27). The kind of family struggle and sibling rivalry that Jacob had demonstrated himself so adept at negotiating in his parental home had now come to roost in his home. As always, such dysfunctional relationships brought a harvest of pain and tears, and Leah was the one who paid the highest price.

But God has a special concern for those whose lives are particularly difficult, whether or not they have contributed to their situation. In Genesis 16, when Sarah's maidservant Hagar found herself isolated and alone in the desert, she was not entirely an innocent bystander who was caught up in a problem situation through no fault of her own. She had first provoked her mistress through her prideful attitude (Gen. 16:4), and then, when Sarah mistreated her, she ran away from home, abandoning the household upon which the promised blessing of God rested. Her actions had brought her to her situation of need. Nonetheless her cry of distress was still heard by the Lord. In a similar way, although Leah was almost certainly a willing participant in deceiving Jacob, the Lord saw the painful consequences of her actions and was concerned for her. As a result, he opened her womb first, so that she bore a son (Gen. 29:31).

This is good news for those whose lives are a mess. Often we are tempted to think of God as the cosmic traffic cop, waiting at the side of the road of life for us to commit some minor infraction so that he can come down on us with the full weight of the law. In reality, though we deserve to have God throw the book at us—and not just for "minor transgressions"—his mercy and grace turn out to be far greater than we ever hoped. Even when our painful situation is the clear and direct result of our sin, God still cares for us. Like the servant in the parable of Jesus, though we have run up an unimaginable debt before God, he is astonishingly willing to forgive us (Matt. 18:21–35).

The indiscriminateness of God's goodness provides a challenge for our attitudes toward others, however. Though we are eager to receive this grace, we are not always so quick to pass it on. There is a reason why Jesus' parable is called the parable of the unmerciful servant, not the parable of the merciful master. We are slow to measure out mercy to others on the same scale as we have received it. We are slow to forgive and swift to call in the debts we perceive that others owe us.

This outlook can affect our diaconal ministries in the church too. Often in our ministries of mercy, as we provide help to those in need, we like to distinguish between the "deserving poor" and the "undeserving poor." We are happy to help the former group, those who have not significantly contributed to their difficulties: widows and orphans, the abused, and so on. We are often far more reluctant to get involved with the latter group. This group includes drug addicts, alcoholics, and other people whose lifestyle or choices have played a significant part in contributing to the mess their lives are in.

Yet God does not seem to distinguish on the same basis as we do. The gospel comes freely to all of us, even though none of us could claim to deserve its good news. Throughout the Bible, God is concerned for those in need, without discriminating on the basis of responsibility. He sends his rain on the just and the unjust (Matt. 5:45). To be sure, we may sometimes have to withhold help from people because it would enable them to continue in their sinful and self-destructive behavior patterns. As the Book of Proverbs reminds us, there are a number of ways of inflicting poverty on yourself: through laziness (6:10), talk instead of hard work (14:23), self-indulgence (21:17), oppressing the poor (22:16), or stinginess (28:22). A handout given to such people without addressing the root causes of their poverty is no true help. However, our concern for the last, the least, and the lost in society should always err on the side of being overly gracious and generous to all, no matter how the persons concerned arrived in that position. In that way, we will be true children of our heavenly Father (Matt. 5:43–48).

NOTICE ME!

With the birth of her first son, Reuben, Leah felt that she had gained important ground on her rival. As with Hagar, the Lord had looked on her affliction, and the result was a male child. Reuben means "See! A son!" His name embodied Leah's desperate cry for attention from her husband: "Notice me!" She said, "The Lord has seen my misery. Surely my husband will love me now" (Gen. 29:32). In these words, you can hear her pain coming to expression. In our sympathy for her difficult position, however, we shouldn't miss the fact that the idolatry that gripped Leah's heart is also uncovered by these words. Even while she took the Lord's name on her lips, her statement revealed the fact that it was her husband's approval that she regarded as truly essential to a meaningful life, not the Lord's. Without Jacob's love, she felt that her life was over. Without his approval, what did it matter that the Lord had seen her misery and answered her prayers? She viewed God as a useful means to winning what is really important in life, Jacob's affections, not as the One who in and of himself supplies all of the meaning in her life.

This is the essence of idolatry: someone or something other than the living God is occupying the God-shaped space at the core of our being. We were created as worshiping beings, people whose meaning and purpose cannot be derived from ourselves but must come from outside us. There is always someone or something other than ourselves on which we have hung our whole identity or self-worth. If we turn our backs on the true God, we inevitably attempt to fill that void with something else. Whatever we must have instead of, or as well as, the God of the Bible, if life is to have meaning for us—that is our idol. For you, it may be health, comfort, wealth, control, the affection of a particular individual, or any of a thousand and one things. Whatever it is, it is an idol. Idols, however, ultimately never satisfy. In reality, a deep relationship with God and God alone is all we need to possess life in all its fullness (see Ps. 27:4–5).

The same idolatrous orientation was present in Leah's naming of her second and third sons, Simeon and Levi. The name Simeon means "heard," and she affirmed with her lips that the Lord had heard of her unloved status and responded to her with this gift (Gen. 29:33). Yet it is evident that the fact that the Lord had seen and heard her misery counted for little if there was no similar seeing and hearing on the part of Jacob. In the same vein, Levi means "attached," and the verbal root is often used in the Bible to describe outsiders to Israel who became converts. They attached themselves to the Lord and to his community, becoming part of God's people (as, for example, in Isa. 56:6). But the one to whom Leah really longed to be attached was not the Lord. His favor was taken almost for granted. Instead, Leah longed to be attached to her husband, and she was sure that now—finally—he would pay attention to her (Gen. 29:34). Yet what she sought remained outside her grasp. Jacob was still cold-hearted toward her. Her idolatry was frustratingly unsatisfied.

THE BLESSING OF UNSATISFIED IDOLATRY

The pain of an unsatisfied idolatry often serves as the messenger of God to reveal the hidden recesses of our hearts to us. As long as we get what we want and our idol is smiling upon us, it is easy for us to be oblivious to the power our idol has gained over us. Something secondary has taken God's place at the center of our lives, and we may never even recognize that there is a problem. As long as we are healthy, we do not suspect how important it is to our self-worth that we are able to stand up and walk around and control our bodies. As long as we are reasonably comfortable financially, we little guess how much we have come to depend and rely on our money. As long as we are beautiful, we do not understand how central that fact has become to our view of ourselves.

As long as we are able to provide the daily sacrifices that our hungry idols require, they smile on us and bless us and we go our merry way. But when we are unable to make the payments they demand, things turn nasty. When we are no longer healthy or wealthy or beautiful, or when we miss a rung on the career ladder and take a nasty tumble, then our idols start to curse us, and we experience a range of negative emotions such as fear, anger, and despair. In the strength of those negative emotions, we discover the true nature of our idols and the depth of their hold on us. As we are plunged into self-doubt and deep despair, we discover how much stock we have placed in the values and virtues and glittering prizes of this world. In God's grace, a Black Monday meltdown on our internal stock market may be the means he chooses to use to open our eyes to what is going on in our hearts.

Tracing back negative emotions is one of the surest ways to uncover the identity of your idols. What causes you to worry intensely? What makes you inordinately angry? What situations tempt you to despair? Dig a little deeper in those areas, and you will find the signs of your idolatry at work. The thing whose loss or threatened loss is crushing your soul has become your idol. Those negative emotions thereby can become messengers from God, enabling you to identify your idols, a necessary prerequisite for turning from them.

Did Leah have such an experience between the births of her third and fourth sons? Did she come to understand her heart better and thereby arrive at a measure of acceptance of the fact that even though she was not Jacob's beloved, she had something that mattered far more deeply? Perhaps so, since she named her fourth son Judah ("praise," Gen. 29:35), saying, "This time I will praise the LORD." It looked as though her eyes had now turned from her husband to the Lord as the object of her affections.

RACHEL'S RESPONSE

Just when it seemed that Leah might be abandoning her idolatry, however, Rachel relaunched the arms race, driven by her insecurity and idolatry. She feared that her sister's fruitfulness would succeed in stealing away her husband's affections, even though there was no evidence to support her concern. Idolatry is like that. It is not driven by reason or by logic but by deeper forces. In fact, Rachel's rivalry with her sister, not the barrenness itself, made her childless situation unbearable. Sarah and Rebekah were barren far longer than Rachel had been, without showing any of her bitterness. They, however, did not have the same kind of household rivalry to contend with.

What was Rachel's response to her painful predicament? She did not lay it out before the Lord with prayer and weeping, as Hannah later would in Shiloh (1 Sam. 1:2–11). Instead, she angrily confronted Jacob with the unreasoning (and unreasonable) demand, "Give me sons, or I'll die" (Gen. 30:1). She did not know what she was asking for. Ultimately it would be the answer to this plea that killed her, as she died in giving birth to her second son, Benjamin (Gen. 35:18). Sometimes we should be more careful what we ask for. As the country song puts it, "Some of God's greatest gifts are unanswered prayers."

In this case, however, the problem was not so much unanswered prayers as unprayed prayers. When Isaac found that his wife was barren, he prayed for her, and his prayer was finally answered (Gen. 25:21). Jacob, however, responded to his wife's prayerless anger in kind: "Am I in the place of God, who has kept you from having children?" (Gen. 30:2). Instead of gently encouraging Rachel and helping her to bring her concerns to the only One who could help, Jacob passed the blame off himself and onto God with a shrug of his shoulders. Instead of empathizing with her pain and pointing her toward spiritual answers, he said, in effect, "It's not my fault." This is not a model of sensitive, self-sacrificial spiritual leadership in the home.

DESPERATE MEASURES

Rachel's desperation led her to adopt desperate measures. She decided to revisit the Hagar strategy of childbearing (Gen. 16:1–2), even though it had caused such havoc first time around. She sent her maidservant Bilhah in to her husband in her place, on the grounds that any children that resulted from their union would legally be hers (Gen. 30:3).

Why would anyone turn again to the bankrupt strategies of the past? The answer is that if you are desperate enough, any straw seems worth clutching. Any alley that may plausibly lead to a way out seems attractive. Indeed, the Hagar strategy did work up to a point for Rachel. Through her maidservant she received two children she could regard as hers, Dan and Naphtali. The names given to these boys show that she regarded the positive end as proof that God approved of her choice of means. Dan means "he has judged," a statement of her belief that his birth means her vindication by God (Gen. 30:6), while Naphtali's name ("my struggle," Gen. 30:8) is a claim to have triumphed in her struggle with her sister. The narrator of the story, however, ascribes no direct role to God in these births as he does in several of the other births in this chapter. Rachel's claims to divine help are left unsupported.

Stung by the recognition of the fact that she had stopped having children and her sister was gaining on her, Leah adopted the same strategy her sister had done. She sent in to Jacob her servant Zilpah (Gen. 30:9). She too saw this strategy succeed in the form of two more sons on her side of the equation through Zilpah. These she named Gad ("fortunate," Gen. 30:10) and Asher ("blessed," Gen. 30:13), claiming that God's favor rests upon her. Once again, however, the narrator is silent as to God's direct involvement in these conceptions.

The low point in this messy soap opera comes in the next section. Leah's son Reuben went out into the fields and found some mandrakes, a plant historically associated with fertility (Gen. 30:14). As Leah's oldest son, Reuben had much to gain from any improvement in his mother's status in the household, so he took the plants home. Word of his find quickly spread, and it wasn't long before Rachel was in the tent requesting a share of the mandrakes. Not surprisingly, Leah was reluctant to part with her valuable commodity, especially to her chief rival. But Rachel persisted until her sister agreed to trade the mandrakes for a night with Jacob (Gen. 30:15).

The sisters' bitter rivalry has cheapened the marital relationship to the point where Jacob's one-flesh intimacy with his wife has become a commodity to be traded for a food item. In a sense, however, Jacob was again reaping what he sowed when he sought to wrest the birthright from Esau in exchange for a bowl of soup. What goes around is coming back around for Jacob.

Ironically, however, the sister who gave up the artificial fertility aid became pregnant. This is because the Lord alone has the power to open the womb, not the mandrakes. God heard Leah's cries and in response granted her two more sons of her own, Issachar ("wages," Gen. 30:18) and Zebulun ("honor," Gen. 30:20). Yet even this gift of God's grace was misinterpreted by Leah. The reason she gives for the naming of Issachar is that she believes that God has rewarded her for her idolatrous shortcut of presenting her maidservant to her husband. Worse, with the naming of Zebulun she returned to her original idolatrous starting point. "This time my husband will treat me with honor, because I have borne him six sons," she said (Gen. 30:20). The more things change, the more they stay the same. Even those idols we think safely dead and buried have a way of coming back to haunt us over and over again. Like vampires, idols often seem to refuse to stay dead.

BUT GOD . . .

Finally God remembered Rachel (Gen. 30:22). It was not, of course, as if God had forgotten Rachel. However, she needed to be emptied of her pride and privilege before she could be filled. What Jacob could not do for her, what the mandrakes could not do for her, at last the Lord did for her, opening her womb and causing her to bear a son. The Lord had compassion on her need and emptiness and gave her a child. Having a son of her own took away Rachel's disgrace, though there is no evidence that it weakened her competitive spirit with her sister. Joseph's name was a request to the Lord for another son (Gen. 30:24). She still was not satisfied with God's gracious provision, though at least now her request seems directed to the right person.

The language of God remembering someone points to a decisive act on God's part, as at the turning point of the flood in Genesis 8:1. When the time was right, God intervened decisively in the lives of his people and the result was Joseph, the one who ultimately would be used by God to save the lives of all of his brothers. Joseph's birth also brought about a decisive change in Jacob's thinking. It is striking that only after Rachel gave birth to a son did Jacob's thoughts turn homeward. He already had ten sons by his other wife and concubines, but in Jacob's mind none of them counted. For Jacob, Joseph was the child of promise for whom he had been waiting all these years. All his hopes revolved around him. His other children were of no real significance to him. The result of this attitude would later be a repetition of the kind of destructive favoritism that had broken up his family.

Perhaps Jacob justified his preference for Joseph in his heart on spiritual grounds. Surely this one, the firstborn of his one true love, would be the bearer of the promise? But ironically Jacob was wrong in his assessment of the situation. Although Joseph would be greatly used by God to bring deliverance to all his brothers, the Messiah would come through the line of Leah's son Judah. God is no respecter of persons. He chooses the foolish to shame the wise and the weak to shame the strong.

For our part, however, we all too easily judge on the basis of external appearances.

Moreover, it is important in the midst of this messy drama not to lose sight of what God is doing in all of this. Human sin and rivalry have been driving the action at one level, but at another level God has been accomplishing his purpose of making Jacob the father of a multitude of sons. What is more, at this point in God's plan the blessing will not pass to either Judah or Joseph. There was not one winner and eleven losers in the race for the Abrahamic blessing. Now the channel of God's blessing was broadening out, even as Isaac had declared in blessing Jacob (Gen. 28:3). God was making Jacob into a company of peoples, and even the sordid scheming of his wives would be the providential means by which God would accomplish his purpose of granting Jacob many sons. At the end of Jacob's life, he would not have to choose only one among his sons to bless, as his father had done; there would be blessings enough for all of Jacob's children to share (Gen. 48–49). Of course, many things might have been easier if Leah and Rachel had worked together harmoniously in pursuit of God's glory from the outset. Much pain might have been avoided. But God's plans were in no way thwarted by their stubborn, self-serving strategizing. On the contrary, it was through their sin that he achieved his good purposes.

ANOTHER NAME

The sorry tale of Jacob's wilderness years and domestic infighting point us back to what is central in the life of Jacob. If Abraham was the man who exemplified faith, Jacob exemplifies grace. In Jacob, God's love was extended to the unlovely sinner, promising great things to him at Bethel—not because of the kind of person he was but in spite of it. This same love was then gradually working in his heart through many painful experiences to make him more than he once was. Jacob is no hero, and his family dynamics do not provide models to be copied. Yet he provides a classic study of the way in which our God specializes in rescuing losers and in redeeming hopeless cases.

The ultimate solution for all of us is not found among any of Leah's or Rachel's sons. It is to be found in another name, the ultimate offspring of Jacob, the true Israelite, Jesus. He is God's one and only Son, who lived up to the name the angel assigned to him: "You are to give him the name Jesus, because he will save his people from their sins" (Matt. 1:21). As Peter declared in Acts 4:12, this name is the only name given to humankind whereby we may be saved. He is the One who brings hope to the hopeless, rest to the weary, and new life to the lost. He brings life even to those, like Leah and Rachel, who are hopelessly lost in their idolatries.

He does so because he came and lived a flawless life in our place. As we stand before God as his children, he looks upon us with love because we come in Jesus' name. As he looks at us, he no longer sees us marred by the kind of jealousies and insecurities that this chapter of Scripture records, even though we too continue to struggle against the cherished idolatries of our hearts. In Christ, however, those sinful thoughts and actions have been covered by his perfect goodness, which enables us to stand before God, accepted in his grace. Christ's spotless record has been given to us. With Jesus, it is not "Give me sons, or I'll die." Rather, it is "Father, I died to win for you these sons and daughters." Hallelujah! What a Savior!

As a result of achieving such an awesome salvation for his people, Jesus is justly exalted to the highest place and given the name above every name (Phil. 2:9). His glorious name is worthy of all praise and adoration. Every knee shall bow before him, and every tongue will confess that Jesus Christ is Lord to the glory of God the Father. All creation will join in the song of praise. That gospel good news is what forms the heart of our worship Sunday by Sunday and what will drive our hearts onward in worship for all eternity.

FOR FURTHER REFLECTION

1. God has a particular concern for the unlovely and the unloved. How can we demonstrate a similar concern in our churches and lives?
2. The names Leah and Rachel gave their children exposed their idolatries. How can we identify the clues that will lead us to our idolatries?
3. How can an unfulfilled idolatry be a blessing? Is that something you have experienced? How?
4. What is God's answer to Rachel's and Leah's idolatry?
5. How can God fulfill his purposes through such great idolaters?

7

DON'T GET MAD, GET EVEN

(GENESIS 30:25-31:55)

The Golden Rule comes in two forms. The Christian version runs like this: "Do unto others as you would have them do unto you." The secular version goes like this: "Do unto others whatever they have done to you, only double." Or, to put it more concisely, "Don't get mad, get even." That's why these days, when you get fired from a job, the security guard comes and watches while you clear out your desk and then escorts you out of the building. They are afraid you might do something they would regret, like programming a bug into the corporate computer system, or worse, deliberately breaking the coffee machine. It's dangerous to rip off your employees too much, to push them too far. That's especially true if you've employed someone like Jacob. Here we see another classic if unedifying conflict between deceiver and deceiver, with Laban and Jacob seeking to outdo the other.

HARD BARGAINING

It started out straightforwardly enough. Now that his favorite wife, Rachel, had borne him a son, Jacob got itchy feet for home. He wanted to return to the Promised

Land with his family (Gen. 30:25). Laban, however, wanted him to stay, not out of family concern but out of commercial motives. He had noticed that having Jacob around had been good for business. By divination, he said, he had discovered that the Lord had blessed him on Jacob's account (Gen. 30:27). In an apparent fit of generosity, he therefore invited Jacob to name his wages.

Jacob did not immediately reply to Laban's offer. Perhaps he remembered what happened last time Laban told him to name his wages (Gen. 29:15). On that occasion he ended up getting the raw end of the deal. Instead, Jacob underlined the fact that Laban's flocks had grown because of his hard work as well as because of divine intervention (Gen. 30:29–30). In his response to Laban, Jacob stressed the second person pronoun, "you *yourself* know," in a way that suggests that he thought that divination ought hardly to have been necessary. There was no mystery to the secret of Laban's success. Common sense alone should have told Laban that Jacob was more than worthy of his keep. But Jacob had gained nothing out of his Herculean labors. When would he get a chance to look after his family interests (Gen. 30:30)?

Laban then meekly reiterated his offer: "What shall I give you?" Again, perhaps mindful of Laban's last gift to him (Leah instead of Rachel), Jacob knew that he needed to examine any gift horses from Laban extremely closely to make sure they weren't of the Trojan variety. He claimed that he didn't want Laban to give him anything; he would prefer to be able to keep part of what he earned (Gen. 30:31). His proposal to Laban was straightforward enough in its broad outlines, if also difficult enough to unravel in all its details to keep generations of commentators arguing. In essence, Jacob wanted all the unusually colored animals in the flock—the black sheep and speckled goats, which would naturally be a small proportion of the whole—while Laban could have the rest. It seemed to be a fair deal; statistically speaking, a roughly consistent percentage of the flock would belong to Jacob. If the flock got bigger, both would benefit. If it got smaller, both would suffer. The different coloration criteria would make it fairly easy to divide the flock and identify each man's share without dispute.

The trouble was that Laban had no intention of leaving it to statistics. The ambiguities in the fine print of Jacob's proposal—such as the question of who would own the initial stock of colored animals—presented an irresistibly wide-open door for a shyster like Laban. Like a skilled corporate lawyer, Laban hastened to sign on to the vague agreement, which he could then interpret to his advantage (Gen. 30:34). Before Jacob had a chance to take inventory, Laban immediately separated out all of the animals that fitted Jacob's description and hid them away with his sons, three days from the flocks that were in Jacob's keeping (Gen. 30:35–36). He must have chuckled at his cleverness in pulling over yet another one on his naïve nephew. With all the oddly colored parents removed, now there would be hardly any oddly colored offspring for Jacob to claim.

Jacob was not so easily defeated, however. He responded with a complex strategy involving strange practices with branches and selective breeding (Gen. 30:37–42). The exact methodology employed is not clear in the text, but the result is. The upshot was that Jacob grew rich at Laban's expense. Deceiving Laban had been outmaneuvered at his own game. The two things that attracted Jacob when he first arrived in Paddan Aram twenty years earlier—Rachel and the flocks—had, after a long and convoluted struggle, finally become Jacob's.

LONGING FOR HOME

Jacob's victory in the battle of wits with his uncle was not without its cost, however. It came at the expense of good relationships with Laban and his family. The narrator notes wryly, "Jacob noticed that Laban's attitude toward him was not what it had been" (Gen. 31:2). What a masterful understatement! I wonder why not? Deceit always leaves a sour residue. It was perhaps not surprising, then, that all of a sudden Jacob got the renewed urge to return to the Promised Land.

Where did that urge come from? First, it came from those bad relationships. Jacob saw that Laban's attitude to him is not what it had been, and so he started to think about leaving. How easy it is when we are comfortable in life to settle down and put down roots as if this world were our home. If everything had gone well between him and Laban, Jacob might never have left Paddan Aram. But times got difficult, and so he started to think about home.

Don't miss the significance of the fact that it is at the point of difficulty that God's call to go home comes to Jacob. That truth goes against the grain for us. Invariably we want life to be easy and smooth. We pray and we plan as far as we can to make life go that way. We beg God to make our lives plain sailing. But sometimes the best way for God to get our attention and move us on to new levels of obedience is through a breakdown of our comfort.

In my experience, I went through a difficult time while I was still working in the oil industry. I was assigned to a department in my company that had no need for me or work for me to do, so I spent a long three months straightening paper clips and doing other tasks of similar importance. That spell of boredom led me to question what I was doing and to look into the possibility of using my engineering gifts in a short-term missions context. Nine months later, I was on a plane to West Africa to work as an electrical engineer for a Christian radio station and hospital, a life-changing experience in many ways. Ironically, by the time I left to go to Africa, I had been transferred by the oil company to work on a different project that I found far more stimulating and fulfilling. Had I been assigned directly to that project at an earlier point, I might never have thought of going overseas.

(MIS)READING PROVIDENCE

Of course, we can easily misread providence. Boredom and even pain do not necessarily signal the fact that God is telling us to move. Sometimes God's plan for us is to persevere faithfully in the midst of frustration and difficulty. But in Jacob's case, to remove any possible doubt, God spelled out his direction clearly in a dream (Gen. 31:10–13). God told Jacob that it was time to pack up and go back home. It was in a dream that Jacob had first met God at Bethel (Gen. 28:12), and now that form of guidance is renewed. In addition, God also made it clear in the dream that all of Jacob's complicated and convoluted breeding strategies in the previous chapter had availed him nothing. It was not his clever plan and hard work that had made him rich but God's blessing. He had prospered because God, the God whom he had met at Bethel, had fulfilled the promise made to him there to be with him and to bless him (Gen. 31:10–13). His brilliant plan could never have succeeded unless God had also had a plan for him.

This is an important lesson for us too. How easy it is for us to trust in our clever ideas and strategies—some of which are even more far-fetched than Jacob's breeding sticks—and to give them the credit for our prosperity and success. If we have invested well in the stock market or reared obedient children or developed a successful church ministry or program, we are easily tempted to take the credit for it. Christian bookstores are inundated with ideas and formulas guaranteed to develop your spiritual life and to grow churches, ideas that range from good medicine to quack remedies. Yet the Bible reminds us that all our labor and ingenuity and effort will be in vain unless the Lord builds the house (Ps. 127:1). Even when the watchmen do what they ought to do and keep good watch, their faithful labor will be wasted unless the Lord guards the city. We are so quick to think when things are going well that it is our cleverness that has achieved our goals. Nonsense! God is accomplishing his purposes through us, and he deserves all of the credit.

In Jacob's situation, God was not only faithfully fulfilling the promise to bless Jacob and be with him; he was also seeking to teach Laban a lesson and was using Jacob as his instrument of judgment (Gen. 31:12). The Lord told Jacob, "I've seen what Laban has been up to, and I have intervened to deliver you." Jacob need not have feared that Laban's ability to exploit legal loopholes would win him the ultimate victory. As the poet once put it, "Though the mills of God grind slowly, yet they grind exceeding small." Do you fear that someone you know is getting away with it and that you will be wronged as a result? Don't be afraid. No one ultimately gets away with anything before God. You can safely leave the matter in his hands to deal with.

LEAVING LABAN

But if it was God's time to leave, the manner of leaving was pure Jacob. He owed Laban nothing. He had God's call to go and his promise of protection. Yet he slid away like a fugitive (Gen. 31:20). He summoned his wives to meet him in the fields, where he could be sure of private conversation. There he laid out the situation before them, in effect asking them to choose sides. Are they with him or with their father? Rachel and Leah, for once operating together, opted to stay with Jacob, although it has to be said that their motivation seems to have been based more on financial calculation than romantic attachment. Here there is no declaration of undying love and commitment, such as we see from Ruth to

Naomi (Ruth 1:16–17). Rather, the women saw no future for themselves with their father, who had treated them like chattels, selling them to Jacob in return for fourteen years of labor and consuming the proceeds (Gen. 31:14–16). Though Jacob won their vote, they do not sound as though they think the match their father arranged for them was the catch of the century.

Rachel was determined not to leave home empty-handed, however. While Laban was away shearing the flock, Rachel did a little fleecing of her own, carrying off Laban's household idols (Gen. 31:19). Why should Rachel have been drawn to this particular piece of household property rather than something more marketable, like silver or jewelry? It appears that Rachel wanted to have all of her bases covered. By stealing the domestic gods, she thought to gain a (pagan) blessing, just as her husband had earlier stolen the true blessing. Perhaps she thought that possession of the idols might improve her chances of safely bearing more sons for Jacob. After all, she had already shown a partiality to the superstitious use of artificial aids to conception (Gen. 30:14). If that was her goal, though, her plan backfired. The idols became so much useless and dangerous baggage on the journey, as Laban pursued the family looking for them (Gen. 31:30–32). Later they probably ended up with the other idols, unceremoniously buried by the oak at Shechem like the trash they were (Gen. 35:2–4).

How much are our lives also cluttered by attachments to similar things? We easily fall in love with objects that weigh us down on our journey through life and end up moth-eaten, rusted, stolen, or buried in a landfill. These are the domestic idols of our day. We think that we cannot do without them—yet one day soon, willingly or unwillingly, we will have to leave them behind. On that day, the true nature of our treasure will be revealed, and only that treasure which is stored up in heaven will last (Matt. 6:19–21). In the light of that reality, are you traveling suitably light?

Rachel was, she thought, looking out for her earthly future. Yet how different are her actions from the behavior of her aunt, Rebekah! Rebekah went off to the Promised Land with nothing, abandoning her share in Laban's family for the sake of an unknown future, by faith. Rachel was going to that same Promised Land with Jacob. But she wanted to take along with her a plan B, a little insurance policy in case things didn't work out. If Rebekah is the picture of faith, surely Rachel is the picture of *us*, isn't she? Like her, we are a mass of contradictions. Like her, we are often found going to the right place but doing it all wrong. Like us, she has faith, but that faith is often almost overwhelmed by her unbelief— or rather her preference for being able to control her destiny by her cleverness. She is a true match for Jacob. Only grace could hold out hope for such a family.

AN AWKWARD FAREWELL

When Laban finally caught up with Jacob and his family, God graciously intervened again. He appeared to Laban in a dream, warning him not to touch Jacob (Gen. 31:24). So when Laban finally overtook Jacob there was an angry scene but nothing worse. Laban's first complaint to Jacob concerned the manner of Jacob's departure. If Jacob had to go, he said, it should have been with a rousing send-off party, thrown for them by Laban (Gen. 31:27). He was right, of course; Jacob should have been sent off to the Promised Land in style by his uncle. However, if you believe Laban's claim that he would have acceded so easily to a simple request from Jacob to leave, then I'd like to talk to you about investing in a nice piece of oceanfront property in Arizona. . . .

Next Laban raised the stickier topic of his mislaid idols. One wonders why Jacob didn't retort to Laban, "What use to you are your idols if they can't even save themselves from being stolen?" But since Jacob was not aware of Rachel's theft, he instead responded with aggrieved innocence: "But if you find anyone who has your gods, he shall not live" (Gen. 31:32). In the light of that statement, we hold our breath as the search closes in on Rachel's tent. But it turns out that we needn't have worried. Rachel was a fitting wife for Jacob and a fitting daughter for Laban, craftier than both of them. She took the idols and hid them in a camel's saddle, which doubled as a kind of couch, and then lay on them (Gen. 31:34). When her father came in and felt all around his younger daughter's tent looking for his lost idols, his sense of touch let him down, just as Isaac's had done when his younger offspring, Jacob, earlier deceived him (Gen. 27:21–22).

To prevent Laban searching in the crucial place, Rachel claimed that she could not get up because "the manner of women" was upon her (Gen. 31:35 NASB). This is normally taken as a reference to menstruation, but in the ancient world menstruating women were rarely confined to bed unable to stand, any more than they are in the modern world. Perhaps she was alluding to the fact that she was already pregnant with Benjamin—a difficult pregnancy would have provided a rather more convincing cover for her inability to stand up. Whatever the precise nature of her excuse, it was sufficient to throw her father off the trail. But although the idols remained safely undiscovered, Jacob's curse was nonetheless strangely prophetic. Within a few months Rachel would be dead, expiring in the course of giving birth to Benjamin (Gen. 35:16–18). The idols brought her nothing but trouble.

CHOOSING A GOD TO SWEAR BY

Against all the odds, however, in spite of the trickery of Jacob and the trickery of Laban, they ultimately departed from one another in peace, establishing a covenant between them. The making of this covenant marks a change in their relationship. They were no longer employer and employee, patron and client, but now were two equals.

Yet there is also something uneven about the way that covenant is formulated. Laban framed it in the form of his religious understanding, swearing by the God (or gods) of Abraham *and* the God (or gods) of Nahor (Gen. 31:53). Laban thought of these authorities as distinct and plural gods, as the plural verb form in the Hebrew shows. It seems that Laban's gods were the gods of way out there and way back when. He swore, if you like, by Grandma and Grandpa's gods, the generic gods of his culture. Jacob, however, took his oath not in the name of the gods of Abraham's father but the God of Abraham's son, Isaac, his father. So he swore by the Fear of his father Isaac (Gen. 31:53), the God of his experience at Bethel, the God who had been watching over him the whole time (Gen. 31:42).

Perhaps this God was not yet fully the God of Jacob. Jacob's experience of God was not yet complete. But he at least recognized him as the God who has intervened in history in a real way. He followed the God who had called Abraham to leave his country and go to the Promised Land, who had chosen Isaac to carry that promise, and who had called Jacob to bear that promised blessing and had been with him on his journey. That calling was not something to be borne lightly, nor was that relationship one of chummy equality. This God is an awesome God; hence the appropriateness of the name the Fear of Isaac. This is a God who is capable of demanding the greatest sacrifice of all, the sacrifice of a beloved only son. Jacob's awareness of God was a far more personal experience than that of his uncle Laban.

What about you? Do you have a vague belief in the god of Grandma and Grandpa, the generic Judeo-Christian god of our culture, whom you may worship at the church or synagogue of your choice? Do you reverence a deity on whom you call only in times of crises or solemnity—weddings, funerals, and sicknesses? Or do you worship the God who has broken into history decisively and personally in Jesus Christ? Do you follow the God who confronts you and me personally with the call to repent and give our lives over to him? Do you serve the God who commands you to give up your small ambitions and lay everything before him on the altar, just as Abraham did with Isaac, the God who will accept nothing less than total commitment? Do you know the character of the God of the Bible well enough to fear him? After all, the Book of Proverbs tells us that "the fear of the LORD is the beginning of knowledge" (Prov. 1:7). Do you fear this God well enough to serve him and obey him, even when it is costly?

The God whom we fear for his awesome magnificence and holiness is also the God whom we love for his equally awesome grace, however. He is a God who is to be loved as well as feared. We love this God, for we have come to know him not simply as the Fear of Isaac but as the God and Father of our Lord Jesus Christ, and we have seen in the cross the place where his fearsome wrath and his abundant mercy meet.

You see, unlike Jacob, who went out into the wilderness with nothing and through the blessing of God there became rich, the Lord Jesus left behind the glories of heaven and for our sakes went out into the wilderness of this sin-stricken world with nothing. There he faced all of the temptations and trials of this earthly existence without resorting to deceit and trickery, without accumulating idols. Then, at the cross, he took upon himself the wrath of God and the curse that we deserved for our idolatry, deceit, and trickery, for our failure to fear and reverence our God as we ought. There at the cross, God made the greatest sacrifice of all, the sacrifice of his one, beloved

Son. Why? So that lost wanderers like Jacob and Rachel, and you and me, might be forgiven and might have life in all its fullness. So that our sins might be laid on him and atoned for once and for all, and so that his righteousness might be gifted to us to enable us to stand in God's presence. So that in him sinners like us might be added to God's people and enabled to call this awesome, majestic, and fearful God our God forever and ever. As William Edwards's translation of the great Welsh hymn by William Rees put it:

> Here is love vast as the ocean,
>   loving kindness as the flood:
> When the Prince of life, our ransom,
>   shed for us his precious blood.
> Who his love will not remember?
>   Who can cease to sing his praise?
> He will never be forgotten
>   throughout heaven's eternal days.
>
> On the mount of crucifixion,
>   fountains opened deep and wide;
> Through the floodgates of God's mercy
>   flowed a vast and gracious tide.
> Grace and love, like mighty rivers,
>   poured incessant from above.
> Heaven's peace and perfect justice
>   kissed a guilty world in love.

FOR FURTHER REFLECTION

1. Why does God sometimes make life difficult for us? How can we tell what he is saying to us through difficulty?
2. How do we sometimes seek to take the credit for God's blessings?

3. What objects (idols) have you taken along on your journey through life? How have they brought you trouble?
4. How is Rachel a fitting wife for Jacob? Is this a punishment for Jacob, or an opportunity to see himself more clearly?
5. How do our names for God and the way in which we address him reveal what we believe about who he is?

8

THE GREAT CONTENDER

(GENESIS 32)

Amazing grace, how sweet the sound that saved a wretch like me." So goes the hymn we love to sing. It all sounds so wonderfully comforting and cozy. But how does grace save a wretch like Jacob? Is salvation always such a sweet and gentle experience, an alluring whisper of grace? Or is it sometimes more like a wrestling match in which God's amazing grace lays hold of you and will not let you go, no matter how hard you struggle? Jacob's experience falls into the latter category. He is not so much sweetly drawn by grace as overpowered by it, as Genesis 32 bears eloquent witness.

GOING HOME

The chapter dawned full of promise for Jacob. His wilderness years were nearly over. His conflict with Laban had reached a peaceful resolution. Jacob was on his way home to the Promised Land. But before he arrived there, there was the little matter of his relationship with brother Esau that needed to be settled. In fact, in order to be reconciled to Esau, Jacob made a significant detour on his journey. It is not so much that geographically Jacob needed to get past Esau on his way back to Canaan. He could probably have found a route that would have avoided the difficult encounter. But even though physically he could have found another way, spiritually he needed to get past Esau before he could enter the land of promise. Past sins cannot be ignored as if they had never happened. They must be dealt with properly before progress can be made. True repentance requires not merely inward sorrow but outward restitution and restoration of damaged relationships, wherever possible.

As he set out on his journey, Jacob received encouragement at the start. He encountered a vision of the angels of God (Gen. 32:1). In the Hebrew, numerous verbal connections link Jacob's experience at Mahanaim back to his former vision at Bethel (Gen. 28). His wilderness years are thus bracketed by these two visions of angels, a drawing back of the veil that enabled him to recognize God's unseen presence with him throughout the intervening period. Here was not only the camp of Jacob but also the camp of God (Gen. 32:2). God is present with his people in the midst of these struggles. As the psalmist put it:

> The angel of the LORD encamps around those
> who fear him,
> and he delivers them. (Ps. 34:7)

Do you see the message that God is trying to get across to Jacob? It is that he need not resort to slippery strategies in the face of obstacles, no matter how overwhelming they appear. Instead, he should trust in the unseen forces of God. Just as God had protected him against the wrath of Laban, so he could be trusted to protect him against any threat from Esau.

That is a tough lesson for all of us to learn, I suspect. How often do you and I take account of the unseen forces that are working behind the scenes to establish God's plans? We are easily overwhelmed by the opposition we can see, and we so easily forget the unseen hosts of the Lord. Like Elisha's servant, we need to have our eyes opened to see past the horses and chariots of our earthly opponent to the horses and chariots of fire that are all around us (2 Kings 6:15–17). If only we really understood, with Elisha, that "those who are with us are more than those who are against us," or to put it in the language of the apostle John, "the one who is in you is greater than the one who is in the world" (1 John 4:4). Armed with that assurance, we would be ready to take on the world for God and to overcome. Our natural preference is to have a visible army defending us rather than an invisible one, but such is not the nature of our spiritual experience. Here we live by faith, the substance of things hoped for, the assurance of things unseen (Heb. 11:1). So too must Jacob.

FAITH PUT TO THE TEST

Jacob's newfound faith in God's presence with him was soon put to the test. He sent out his messengers to his brother, Esau, just as he had earlier received God's messengers (Gen. 32:3; in Hebrew the word for "messenger" and "angel" is the same). They went bearing gifts and a carefully crafted message of repentance. Jacob described himself as "your servant" and Esau as "my lord." He thus voluntarily reclaimed the position of subordinate younger brother, which he had schemed and worked so hard to get out from in his earlier life. Jacob's only goal was a restoration of his relationship with his brother. He longed that he might find favor in Esau's eyes (Gen. 32:5).

The reply that came back to Jacob seemed ominous, however. Esau was coming to meet him with four hundred men (Gen. 32:6). This did not sound like a hearty welcome home from a brother who has forgiven and forgotten. Instead, it sounded more like a small to medium-sized army, brought to teach Jacob a lesson once and for all. What was Esau planning now?

Put yourself in Jacob's shoes. Imagine the thoughts that would have been racing through his brain. Perhaps there were thoughts like, Why is this happening to me? Why is everything going so horribly wrong? Here I am, going out of my way to set things straight, and now this! It would have been better if I had let the old enmity linger on undisturbed and had never tried to put our relationship right!

It is intensely painful to have your intentions misunderstood, isn't it? It is so hard to be trying to do the right thing and resolve broken relationships and then to have it all blow up in your face. Yet isn't it only at such times that you find out *why* you are trying to do the right thing? Are you trying to do the right thing because you think it will make your life more comfortable? Are you trying to do the right thing to ease a guilty conscience? Or are you doing it because it is the right thing to do? Are you seeking to do what God has commanded in his Word because you want to please him above everything? If your prime motivation is to please God, then you will persevere in doing the right thing even when it brings you nothing but trouble and persecution.

PRESSING ON, WITH PRAYER

The key point to notice is that, even faced with the apparent prospect of imminent disaster, Jacob didn't give up. He didn't turn around and flee for his life. In spite of his fear and distress, he continued on into the lion's den. That is not to say that Jacob had abandoned strategy. He adopted a practical plan, dividing his family into two groups in hopes that if one were to be attacked, the other might escape (Gen. 32:8). Perhaps if he had remembered the other second camp, the unseen camp of God's angels, he would have been less concerned for the safety of his two camps. But now, in addition to his plan, he prayed (Gen. 32:9). This is the first time we have seen Jacob praying. Finally he was learning that strategy alone is not enough.

Jacob's prayer began with an affirmation of God's past faithfulness to his promises (Gen. 32:9). He recognized that God had more than fulfilled everything he had said he would do for Jacob in Genesis 28. At the same time, Jacob also proclaimed his unworthiness of God's favor (Gen. 32:10). It is hardly a coincidence that Jacob proclaimed himself God's servant for the first time on the same day he declared himself to be Esau's servant. Jacob had come to see that in God's program, growing means becoming smaller. As Jesus put it, "If anyone wants to be first, he must be the very last, and the servant of all" (Mark 9:35). Greatness in his kingdom is a gift God gives to the humble, not a prize to be grasped by the proud.

The essence of Jacob's plea to God in his prayer was that God would continue to fulfill his promises to him (Gen. 32:12). Isn't that always the best approach to prayer in such difficult situations? What do you do when it seems that everything is going wrong, even though we are trying our utmost to do what is right? You lay out all of your fears before the Lord, ask him to do what he has committed himself to do in his Word, and then press on in faith.

A STRANGE ANSWER

The answer to Jacob's prayer came in a strange way, however. He had sent everyone else on ahead of him, across the river. Meanwhile, he planned to spend the night alone, presumably preparing his heart in prayer for the frightening day to come (Gen. 32:23). He had done everything humanly possible to prepare the way for himself, sending a caravan of gifts ahead of him (Gen. 32:13–21). These gifts were designated *minchah*, a Hebrew word that means more precisely "tribute," offerings made by an inferior to a superior. The catalog of Jacob's gifts is overwhelming: herds of goats and sheep, camels and donkeys, underlining the depth of Jacob's self-humiliation. Then, after all of these gifts, would come Jacob (Gen. 32:20). The "me first" brother was finally content, even eager, to be last.

But before Jacob met Esau, first he had to meet God. What an encounter, though! God appeared before him in the form of a man and wrestled with him (Gen. 32:24). God literally assaulted him! What a strange way to deal with a man already scared out of his wits. We may picture Jacob quietly standing there praying for peace in his heart and then—boom!—a stranger appeared from nowhere and knocked him over. Immediately he was involved in a life-and-death struggle, a struggle that he could not win and that he was determined not to lose. Even when the struggle crippled his hip and he could do no more than cling onto his adversary, he did just that and would not let him go until he received from him a blessing (Gen. 32:26).

WRESTLING FOR THE BLESSING

In this encounter is encapsulated the story of Jacob's life. He had made a career out of extracting a blessing from the most unpromising of circumstances. He must have that blessing, no matter what! However, this time—for the first time—Jacob was finally forced to seek the blessing in the right place, from God.

What is the point of this strange incident? Why did God deal with Jacob in that rough-and-tumble fashion? There was a lesson that Jacob needed to learn. All of his life, Jacob had been struggling and striving against human opposition. The cards had been stacked against him, yet through his craftiness he had often come out on top. Behind him, however, he had left a trail of broken relationships and a history of running away when the place got too hot. He had been afraid of what people could do to him. What Jacob needed to learn was that all of his struggling against men had got him nowhere because the one with whom he must ultimately struggle is God. It was not Esau who could prevent him entering the Promised Land; only God could do that. It is not Esau he must fear; it is God he must fear.

In this struggle with God, there are two keys to understanding Jacob's success. He doesn't give up, and he doesn't run away. God was testing his commitment to the promise. It would have been easy for Jacob to say, "Even God seems to be against my return to the Promised Land. I give up! Let me just go and live out my life somewhere in peace." But he didn't do that. Even when everything was stacked against him, Jacob clung to obedience and to the call he had received to return to the Promised Land. He must have God's promised blessing, even though he die in achieving it.

Does God ever deal with us like that? I think sometimes he does. Sometimes he calls us to serve him in some way—and then for the longest time he seems to have forgotten all about us. Everything comes crashing down about our ears, as if God were determined to destroy us. What do you do in times like that? You cling tighter to God and to his promises. All of Jacob's strength, even his very strength to walk, had to be broken down by God, so that Jacob could see that all he could do is cling to God and seek a blessing from him. So that was what he did. He didn't give up. He didn't run away. He clung tighter. In return, he received God's blessing and a new name, Israel, because he had struggled with God and with men and had overcome (Gen. 32:28).

In some ways, Jacob's experience was parallel to that of Job. Remember how God allowed Satan to take away all of Job's wealth, all of his children, all of his health? Then Job's wife said to him (paraphrasing), "Why don't you just curse God and die? It's obvious that God is against you. He is determined to blot you out. Why don't you give up the unequal struggle?" (Job 2:9). But Job wouldn't. Instead, he replied, "Should we accept good from God, and not trouble?" (Job 2:10). He said, "Though he slay me, yet will I hope in him" (Job 13:15). It was not easy for Job to say that. In the context of his sufferings, these were not trite slogans. The whole book is a record of his struggle with God. He never received the answer to why all these things had happened to him. But he met God; he submitted himself to God; he never ran away.

How about you and me? Are we ready to wrestle with God? Do we trust him enough to cling to him even if he seems to have turned against us? Or are we ready to follow him only if he rolls out the red carpet for us? There are no promises in his Word of such red-carpet treatment. On the contrary, we are given the assurance of afflictions and trials throughout our lives. Jesus promised us troubles—but along with those troubles a peace that overcomes (John 16:33)!

A NEW NAME: ISRAEL

Jacob's new name, Israel, is just that: a radically new name, marking a radical change in his nature. Unlike Abram/Abraham and Sarai/Sarah, his new name is not a variant and an extension of what has gone before but rather a transformation. His lifelong attempt to gain the promised blessing by ingenuity and striving rather than by grace had now to be abandoned. But perhaps because that sanctifying transformation is partial in all of us in this life, so also was Jacob's name change. Unlike Abraham and Sarah, who, once given their new names, never reverted to their old ones, Jacob was from now on Jacob *and* Israel. The biblical text alternates between the two designations for the patriarch not because it comes to us from two different sources, as scholars have sometimes argued, but because Jacob/Israel has two warring natures. In the language of Martin Luther he is *simul justus et peccator*—at the same time justified and a sinner. God's work is established in principle in his life, as the new name Israel clearly declares, but it would take a lifetime for that principle to work itself out in fullness. As long as he lived on earth, part of him would still be Jacob.

That new name, Israel, was acquired by Jacob not through success or shrewdness but through enduring the assault of God. It is grace, to be sure, but not the kind of grace we thought that we knew or wanted. Meeting God in this instance did not lead to peace and healing for Jacob but to an enduring, painful crippling. Jacob would forever bear on his body the marks of this painful yet grace-filled encounter with God in which to survive and cling was to triumph. Thereafter his descendants memorialized Jacob's encounter by not eating the meat attached to the socket of the hip (Gen. 32:32).

THE FINAL ISRAEL

How can we miss the connection to the cross? There God the Son endured the agonizing assault of God the Father so that grace and blessing might flow out to his people. Having completed his wrestling with man throughout his earthly life, Jesus Christ wrestled with God on our behalf. He wrestled with God in the garden, crying out, "If it is possible, may this cup be taken from me" (Matt. 26:39). He wrestled with God on the cross, in that awful moment when he cried out, "My God, my God, why have you forsaken me?" (Matt. 27:46). The outcome of his wrestling was not merely that he was crippled in the hip; he was wounded and flogged and crucified and burdened down with the whole weight of our transgressions. But Jesus clung to God and would not let him go unless he received a blessing—not a blessing for himself but a blessing for us, his people. Through his faithful clinging to the Father, he prevailed over sin and death, and as a result he has been given the name above every name.

Jesus is the true Israel, the one who has in fullness struggled with God and struggled with men and has overcome. We in turn become part of the Israel of God as we are united to Christ (Gal. 6:16), participating in his struggles and suffering as well as in his victory. Jesus struggled on the cross not so that you and I might never have to struggle but so that our struggles might be fruitful, making us more like him (Phil. 3:10–11). It is in our struggles and suffering that we are finally taught to abandon our self-dependence and look to the cross, clinging to God alone for blessing. When you fear God, you will have nothing else to fear. Cling to him with all your strength, and you will find that he will not let you go.

What is more, we too are regularly called to memorialize this great battle in our eating, whenever we gather at the Lord's table. There I remember Christ's wrestling on the cross. There I am to remember the tearing apart of his body for me. There I recall the shedding of his blood for my transgressions. There I cling to God and ask him to fulfill his promises to us and in us. There at the table, our souls are fed with God's assurance that no matter what Esaus with their armies may face us in this life, the love of God has laid hold of us and will not let us go. It is a thought that George Matheson's great hymn catches perfectly:

O Love that wilt not let me go,
 I rest my weary soul in thee:

I give thee back the life I owe,
   that in thine ocean depths its flow
May richer, fuller be.

O Light that follow'st all my way,
   I yield my flickering torch to thee;
My heart restores its borrowed ray,
   that in thy sunshine's blaze its day
May brighter, fairer be.

O Joy that seekest me through pain,
   I cannot close my heart to thee;
I trace the rainbow through the rain,
   and feel the promise is not vain,
That morn shall tearless be.

O Cross that liftest up my head,
   I dare not ask to fly from thee;
I lay in dust life's glory dead,
   and from the ground there blossoms red,
Life that shall endless be.

FOR FURTHER REFLECTION

1. Have you ever been overpowered by God's grace? How?
2. Why is it important for you to be aware of the unseen spiritual battle going on all around you?
3. What kind of prayer does Jacob pray in his difficulty? How might you pray a similar prayer in your trials?
4. How and why does God test your commitment to his promises? How does he want you to respond?
5. What difference does it make that we look back to Jacob's wrestling through the cross?

9

CLOSE ENCOUNTERS

(GENESIS 33)

Y ou know the phrase "out of the frying pan, into the fire"? Those words could have been coined to describe Jacob's experience on the far side of the fords of the Jabbok. Of course, some kinds of meeting are never comfortable at any time of day or night. When is it ever a good time to be summoned into the principal's office or to be pulled over by a traffic policeman? So also Jacob could hardly have been looking forward to coming face to face with his old adversary, Esau. He didn't have long to wait. He had no time to rest and gather his strength after his all-night wrestling match with God, no opportunity even to sit down and catch his breath. On the contrary, he had no sooner finished one uncomfortable meeting, his wrestling match with God, than he looked up and found himself in the presence of Esau. As Jacob limped across the river to rejoin his family, there was his brother, whom he had robbed of his birthright, coming to meet him with four hundred men (Gen. 33:1).

SEEING BEYOND THE VISIBLE

To human eyes, it looked a most ominous sight. But Jacob had been prepared by his divine encounter to see beyond the visible. At his last camping place, Mahanaim, he saw the angels around him (Gen. 32:1–2). Since then, he had been accosted by God, who had sought to test his will to return to the Promised Land. Even though it had cost him his health and his strength, Jacob had passed that test. In comparison with that cosmic struggle, a band of four hundred potentially hostile men was chicken feed.

Old habits die hard, to be sure. So Jacob first took care that his favorites, Rachel and Joseph, were safely tucked away at the back of the procession where their chances of escape would be best if everything went horribly wrong (Gen. 33:2). Salvation does not mean instant transformation in any of us. In Jacob's case, the patterns of relating he had learned from his parents, with Rebekah favoring him and Isaac favoring Esau, continued to be replayed with his own children. Joseph's fancy coat of many colors was merely a symptom of the longstanding family patterns that led to his brothers hating him, not the sole cause.

But even though Jacob had not been totally transformed by his encounter with God—he is still Jacob, as well as being Israel—that encounter was not without effect in his life. Whereas before, he had planned to be at the back of the whole procession, this time, after arranging his family, Jacob went out first to meet Esau (Gen. 33:3). Once he had met with God, he could face even the potentially deadly wrath of Esau without fear.

When he encountered Esau, Jacob immediately set about the task of making restitution for the wrongs done to his brother. He bowed down to the ground seven times (Gen. 33:3), a symbol of complete submission and deference. The gifts that Jacob sent to Esau were no mere formal observance of the necessities of oriental culture; they represented Jacob giving back to him the blessing of Genesis 27:28. Jacob was recognizing publicly that the richness of the gifts of heaven and earth that he had experienced belonged properly to Esau. This was an enormously symbolic act for Jacob. Giving Esau these gifts represented for Jacob nothing less than a reversal of a life of stealing from his brother. In addition, bowing down to Esau seven times represented a reversal of the blessing he had illegitimately received from his father in Genesis 27:29: "Be lord over your brothers, and may the sons of your mother bow down to you." Jacob was demonstrating by his deeds that he was truly repentant for what he had done.

Isn't restitution the hardest part of truly biblical repentance? I know it is for me! So often when we have done wrong we want to get by with merely saying sorry, rather than putting things right. If at all possible, we prefer saying sorry directly to God, not even to the other people involved. But biblical repentance means more than saying sorry. It also involves face-to-face confession and restitution, where that is possible. True repentance challenges our pride, as it calls us to humble ourselves, admit our sin, and deal responsibly with the consequences of our actions. That is why we find it so hard. Repentance involves a costly obedience, not merely repeating certain words.

THE PRODIGAL BROTHER'S WELCOME

The impact of Jacob's gesture of repentance on Esau was dramatic. He didn't wait for Jacob to launch into his carefully prepared speech of sorrow for all the ways in which his sins had affected Esau. Instead, he ran to meet him and embraced him, and fell on his neck and kissed him (Gen. 33:4). The similarities to the reception of the prodigal son by his father are suggestive (Luke 15:20). In place of the wrestling and bitter conflict that had characterized Jacob's and Esau's earlier relationship, now there was hugging and joyful weeping. Repentance, though painful and costly, was bearing its fruit.

Though Jacob was careful repeatedly to address his

brother with the deferential address "my lord," Esau in his response named Jacob "my brother" (Gen. 33:9), now not merely a statement of fact but a term of endearment. The prodigal brother was welcomed home with tears. It turned out that Jacob's concerns over Esau's four hundred men were misplaced. Ironically the question that had been tormenting Jacob since he heard of the size of Esau's welcome party, "What do you mean by all these droves [literally, camp] I met?" was found on Esau's lips as a response to the scale of Jacob's gifts (Gen. 33:8). The only army to be seen when the two brothers meet is the army of presents that Jacob had sent to Esau.

Why was Jacob sending these items to his brother? His response to Esau's question was simple: "To find favor in your eyes, my lord." God had already shown Jacob his favor, as Jacob testified in verses 5 and 11; the children and material blessings he had received were gifts of God's grace. But having been reconciled with God, he also wanted to be reconciled to his brother. One without the other was not sufficient. Once again, though, Jacob was remarkably sensitive in his speech to Esau. In describing God's good provision for him, he spoke of God's gracious gift rather than God's blessing—this was not the place to mention that! Instead, he reserved that word to describe his gift to his brother. It was not merely a gift or even the tribute (*minchah*) that a superior might legitimately expect from an inferior, as he names it in Genesis 33:10. Rather, Jacob specifically called what he was giving his brother a blessing (*berakah;* Gen. 33:11). With those flocks, Jacob was giving his brother back the temporal blessings that went with the stolen birthright.

HAS ESAU CHANGED?

But if Jacob was a man who had been changed by his experience of God's grace, as he demonstrated through his repentance, what about Esau? Esau hadn't changed much over the course of these chapters, I'm afraid. Oh, in some ways he was different. He had changed his mind about revenge, for example. He was no longer out to kill Jacob, as he had been last time we met him, in Genesis 27:41. That much was good. But look at the contrast between how Esau described his state and how Jacob spoke of his condition. Jacob said, "God has been gracious to me and I have all I need"; Esau said, "I already have plenty." It's a small difference but a significant one, I think. What Esau is saying to Jacob, in effect, is that God's blessing didn't matter all that much after all; he had managed fine without it.

This impression of the respective orientations of the two men is strengthened as you look at their exchange more closely. Jacob mentioned God three times in their conversation, while Esau didn't mention him once. You get the sense that God didn't enter Esau's picture of the world in any real way, whereas he had become the central reality in Jacob's life. Through his tangled course of life, Jacob had come to realize that the blessing he had experienced was not the result of his cleverness and scheming but of God's graciousness to the undeserving. Esau never learned that lesson.

The difference in perspective between Jacob and Esau makes a big difference in how you approach life, doesn't it? If God is the central reality in your life, then things become merely a means of serving God. Righteousness—obeying and pleasing God—becomes the end. All of God's good gifts are recognized as just that: good gifts. They do not spring from our abilities and efforts, nor are they ours by rights. They are God's to give or to withhold or to repossess as he chooses. My career, my house, my possessions, my spouse, my family, my health, my strength, all of the good things God gives are not my right; they are means to serving the God who gave them—and who has the right to take them away whenever and however he chooses.

That perspective on life is why Jacob was willing to send these expensive gifts to Esau and to persuade him to accept them, even when he seemed willing to decline them, because it was the right thing to do. A right relationship with his brother had become more important to Jacob than material possessions, because such a relationship with our brothers is an implication of a right relationship with our heavenly Father. However, if God is not the central reality in your life, then something else will take control of the center of your being. It may be your possessions, your wealth, your health, a relationship, or some other idol. It may be a noble cause or a degenerate vice. Either way, your life will become turned in on yourself, and you will find yourself willing to do whatever it takes to guard these idols and to achieve the goals that they set for you. The result of that wrong orientation will be the destruction of the relationship not only with your heavenly Father but ultimately also with your earthly brother. Horizontal and vertical relationships cannot be separated.

FACE TO FACE—BUT NOT SIDE BY SIDE

Jacob's new heart for God and for his brother is clearly seen in what he said to Esau in Genesis 33:10: "To see your face is like seeing the face of God." There's a phrase that is packed with meaning. On the one hand, meeting Esau was the goal of his endeavors. He wanted more than anything else in this world to be in a right relationship with the one whom he had wronged. It was as desirable as seeing the face of God. On the other hand, however, seeing the face of God is an extremely dangerous business. Not many people see God and live. That is why in Genesis 32:30 Jacob exclaimed in amazement, "I saw God face to face, and yet my life was spared." Jacob knew that he was taking a similar risk in following through with his determination to put things right with

Esau. His brother had sworn to kill him last time they saw each other. He could in geographical terms have reentered the Promised Land without encountering his brother, but not in spiritual terms. He had to be put right with Esau, and he was willing to risk his life to do it. And lo, wonder of wonders, he not only saw the face of God and lived, he also saw his brother's face and lived to tell the tale. Amazing! What is more, he did so not by his strength, not through some cunning trick, but in weakness and humility, seeking humbly to make restitution for the wrong he had done.

But reconciliation does not always lead to living side by side. Esau apparently wanted Jacob to join him in Seir, outside the Promised Land. Jacob didn't want to go with him there, nor should he have gone with him, given his summons by God to return to the Promised Land. The child of promise cannot go and live alongside those who are outside the line of blessing, who live outside the land of blessing. He was right to refuse Esau's invitation.

However, Jacob seems unwilling to come out directly and tell Esau that he cannot come and live with him. Instead, he formulated a variety of plausible and valid obstacles to Esau's proposals, none of which was entirely relevant (Gen. 33:12–15). Some commentators read into Jacob's mind a plan to go and visit Esau once he has settled in Succoth, but I think that they are probably being too generous to Jacob. I think that this is another area where, though redeemed, Jacob is still not completely pure. Though he gave his brother the impression that he would continue southward to join him in Seir, instead he turned immediately west and settled for a while in Succoth.

SUCCOTH AND STOP OR BETHEL OR BUST?

At Succoth, Jacob built himself a house (Gen. 33:17). Some time later, he moved on from there a short distance to Shechem, thereby arriving safely in the Promised Land. At Shechem, Jacob bought a piece of ground for himself (Gen. 33:18). Our tendency is to skip over these verses as mere filler, a sidetrack from the main story. However, these are not irrelevant travel notices. On the contrary, they are the declaration that God has fulfilled the promise he made earlier to Jacob at Bethel. Jacob has returned safely to the Promised Land (Gen. 28:21), not simply with food and drink for the journey as he requested but with wives and children, flocks and herds. Jacob had received a great abundance through God's gracious and faithful provision.

Since God had thus fulfilled his promises to Jacob, we would expect the next word to be Jacob fulfilling his vows at Bethel. Jacob was almost there. The hard part was over, the bulk of the journey with its greatest dangers had been surmounted. But then he stopped. Jacob had vowed to return and worship at Bethel, the house of God (Gen. 28:22); instead, after being reconciled to Esau, he settled at Succoth and built a house for himself there (Gen. 33:17). The contrast between vow and performance is striking: building a house for himself instead of seeking God's house. Nor do we know how long he dallied there, pursuing his interests instead of God's.

Even when he finally left Succoth and crossed the Jordan, Jacob continued further west, to Shechem instead of turning south to Bethel. Not once but twice, therefore, Jacob stopped short of full obedience to God. Why was that? What was Jacob doing settling down at Shechem and raising an altar when he should have been continuing on to Bethel to raise the altar there, where he had first had the dream? Did Jacob think that Shechem was a better site for trade and for his flocks? Perhaps he thought it didn't matter. After all, Bethel was now a mere twenty miles or so away; he could go there whenever it suited him, once he got settled. Why be so precise in these things? Shechem or Bethel—it's really all the same, isn't it?

Indeed, it is not. Whatever his motivation, Jacob's compromise and his failure to follow through with complete obedience to what he had vowed would cost him and his family dearly, as we shall see in the following chapter. Almost obedience is never enough. Being in the right ballpark may be sufficient when watching a baseball game, but it is not nearly enough when it comes to obeying God. Nothing short of full obedience is required. We all know that intellectually. So why is it, then, that we are so like Jacob, inclined to settle for a halfway house instead of going all the way home to God? Why is it that so often we need a crisis in our lives to move us that short step from almost obedience to full, unreserved obedience?

A WELL-NAMED ALTAR

But if Jacob built his altar in the wrong place, he still gave it a good name. He called it *El elohe yisrael:* the mighty Creator God is the God of Israel—and not the God of the nation Israel, but the God of the person Israel. Now his God was not merely the Fear of Isaac, as he had named him in Genesis 31:53; now he was his God. Jacob/Israel had met that God at Bethel and had heard his words of promise. He had met with that same God at Peniel, where he had faced his power and strength. Over the years of his exile, he had experienced his goodness and provision. This great and mighty and merciful God would be his God, just as he had vowed so many years before at Bethel (Gen. 28:22). Jacob would keep at least that much of the vow.

But where is the might and majesty of this Creator God, the God of Israel, most clearly seen? Isn't it in devising a plan of redemption that can take poor compromised and compromising liars like Jacob and save them? By God's grace, Jacob was changing and becoming Israel.

That is good. There was evidence that God was at work in his life and that he was slowly becoming the new creation he had been called to be. But his salvation would be just as much by grace and not by works at the end of his life as it was at the beginning. God acted in the first place to initiate their relationship. It was God who made a promise to him at Bethel, as he set out on his wanderings; God found him even though he was not seeking for God. More than that, God had picked him out for a special relationship even from the womb. That divine initiative was so profound that God could say, "Yet I have loved Jacob, but Esau I have hated" (Mal. 1:2).

God did not love Jacob because he gave God the credit for the good things that he had and hate Esau because he didn't. On the contrary, out of pure, simple, sovereign grace God chose to reveal himself to Jacob and turn him into Israel, while Esau was left materially comfortable but spiritually unchanged by the touch of God's grace.

THE TRIUMPH OF GRACE

Don't you see? That is how election works—in you and me, just as much as in Jacob. It is all of God's initiative and God's grace, not because of anything in us. How slow we are to recognize that truth! Last summer, I was visiting a different church while on vacation. There we sang a song that focused around the idea of offering all that I am and all that I have to God. There is nothing necessarily wrong with that thought; Romans 12 tells us that we are to offer our bodies as living sacrifices. However, as I looked around me and into my heart, I realized that we naturally tend to sing it as though we expected God to be rather impressed with me and my stuff poured out before him. The reality, however, is that God is not much impressed with who you are and what you have. God saves you and me not because we contribute something valuable to his church and his kingdom. Everything we have comes from him, except for our one, unique contribution to this world: our sin.

It may be true, as the bumper sticker ungrammatically puts it, that "God don't make no junk"; it is also regrettably true that we all do a good job by ourselves of turning our lives into trash. Any time he wished to, God could raise up far more gifted people than you or me out of the stones, who would be able to do far more profound acts of service to him. Yet by his grace he has chosen to save us. He saves us, poor compromised and compromising sinners, not for what we can do for him but out of pure, simple, sovereign grace.

These riches of God's goodness come to you and to me at Christ's expense. For the sake of his brothers, he set aside his glory and might and power. Jesus took on himself the lowest place, the place of the servant, not because that was his proper place as it was for Jacob but so that, having taken the lowest place for us, he might exalt us along with him. His obedience was in no way partial or incomplete, like Jacob's, but was full and perfect, sufficient to bring spiritual blessings upon all those who are his people. It is, in fact, Christ's perfect righteousness and obedience that we offer to God, not our own! When we do so, we present an offering that is truly acceptable to God. It is clothed in Christ's righteousness alone that we are able and welcome to stand before God's throne.

Yes, there should be growth in your life, just as there was in Jacob's. There should be more Israel and less Jacob in each of us day by day. Yes, you should grow in your ability to confess your sins and make restitution. As you do so, your relationships with your earthly brothers will increasingly be restored to peace and fruitfulness. Yes, there are spiritual gifts that God has given to each one to be used for the sake of his people. You are designed by God to be a unique blessing to those around you. No one else can quite fill the space God intended for you. But it is not your growth or your relationships or your gifts that save you. It is God, by his grace alone. Mighty is the God of Israel? You'd better believe it. Mighty indeed is our God.

FOR FURTHER REFLECTION

1. How is repentance different from saying sorry?
2. What is the difference between Esau's attitude to possessions and Jacob's? Which attitude is more like yours? How can you tell?
3. Why do you think that Jacob doesn't go with Esau even after they are reconciled? Does this mean that when we forgive someone, we don't have to forget what he or she has done—or might do?
4. In what ways do you tend to stop short of full obedience to God?
5. Why is it important and encouraging to us to see that Jacob still needs God's grace at the end of his life, just as much as at the beginning?

IO

THE WEAKNESS OF STRENGTH

(GENESIS 34)

What on earth is this whole sorry episode of Dinah and the Shechemites doing in the Bible? If you are reading the Scripture to find inspiring and uplifting stories, this chapter is not what you are looking for. Perhaps that is why this is one of those passages that rarely, if ever, gets preached on. It doesn't appear in children's storybook Bibles, for obvious reasons. Meanwhile, if you happen to come across it as part of your Bible reading in your personal devotions, you will probably say, "Oh, my goodness!" and move on, hoping to find something easier to cope with. Can this really be part of the "all Scripture" that Paul described as inspired by the Holy Spirit and useful to equip the man or woman of God for every good work (2 Tim. 3:16)? If so, what can there possibly be for us to learn from such a sordid affair? This is not exactly a WWJD? ("What would Jesus do?") sort of passage.

THE TRIUMPH OF WEAKNESS

To come to grips with this passage, we must see it in its context. In the previous two chapters, we saw Jacob triumphing in weakness. Jacob has struggled with God and with man and has overcome (Gen. 32:28). He has wrestled with God and survived the face-to-face encounter. He has faced up to his brother, Esau, with four hundred men at his back, has made restitution for a life of stealing and been restored to a relationship with him. In neither case did Jacob go into the situation or emerge from it in a position of strength, yet he triumphed in and through weakness. All that there was left for our hero to do was to ride off happily into the sunset—in his case back to Bethel, as he had vowed—build an altar there, and live happily ever after.

At this point in the story, therefore, we are ready for the happy ending for the prodigal who has come home. His elder brother has run to meet him, has embraced him, has thrown his arms around his neck and kissed him. We are ready for a happy ending that perhaps in this case even involves the elder brother. But it doesn't happen. The story takes an unexpected downward twist. Why doesn't the story go as we expect? Perhaps it is because real life is always more complicated than Hollywood allows for. Real people like us are a complex mass of emotions and desires, and the narratives of our lives are rarely simple and smooth.

Indeed, much great literature captures this sense of the tragedy that is constantly lurking in the shadows of triumph. Margaret Mitchell's novel *Gone with the Wind* provides a classic example. After Rhett and Scarlett have traveled a long and often difficult road, we finally reach the point where their story seems all set for a happy ending—only to be let down with a bump. Instead of Rhett and Scarlett living together happily (if stormily) ever after, Rhett declares that frankly, he doesn't care . . . and then he walks out. As Scarlett cries out fiercely, tomorrow may be another day, but the question is left wide open as to whether the next day will be happy or sad. The course of true life, like the course of true love, rarely runs smoothly.

Why didn't Jacob carry on to Bethel to fulfill his vow? It looks as if the world had taken too strong a hold on Jacob's heart. Jacob was starting to enjoy being in a position of strength, for once. He had become rich, and Succoth perhaps appealed to him because of its spaciousness. Shechem then appealed to him more because of the greater possibilities it offered for trade and business. Jacob was tired of being merely a sojourner, a stranger and an alien like his grandfather Abraham, dealing daily with insecurity, dependent upon the goodwill of others (and God) for his prosperity. Instead of owning only enough of the Promised Land to be buried in (Gen. 23), Jacob wanted to buy some land to live on. Jacob was fed up with struggling. He wanted to retire from his life of wrestling, to settle down in peace and enjoy life, his pilgrimage over. After all, he was back in the Promised Land. His traveling days were done.

THE DANGER OF COMPROMISE

Do you see what is happening? No sooner is Jacob back in the Promised Land than danger arises, the danger of compromise. In order to see the significance of this lesson, we need to remember the audience for whom this story was first written. It was written for the wilderness generation under Moses, those who were about to enter the Promised Land. Do you see the warning there is for them? Look out! For forty years, you have been struggling in the wilderness. It's been a tough road. You feel like you too have been wrestling with God and with man to receive the promised blessing. Soon you will enter the Promised Land. You will be tempted to think that now your journey is over you can relax. Don't do it! Don't let down your guard once you arrive in the land. Catastrophe can strike there too. Here in this world we have no abiding city. As long as we live on this earth, our lives must continually be marked by watchful pilgrimage. We can never feel that we have arrived or that we can settle down and retire. We need to be pressing on continually toward the mark of full obedience.

It is striking to notice that even while Jacob was settling for superficial obedience, his religious activities continued unchecked. He built an altar at Shechem and called it *El elohe yisrael:* the mighty God is the God of Israel. We looked at the positive side of that name in the last chapter. But the purpose for building this altar remains ambiguous. Was it an act of faith on Jacob's part? Or was it rather an act of religious self-deception, an attempt to baptize his halfway obedience? When Jacob, as Israel, proclaims that the mighty Creator God is his God, is he trusting in that mighty God, or is he resting presumptuously on the new name he has been given? God is not Jacob's private God, whom he can call upon wherever and whenever he chooses. God revealed himself to Jacob in the first place not as *El elohe yisrael* but *El bethel,* the God of Bethel. God will not settle for compromised affections. Half a heart will not do for God. In order to stir Jacob's heart up to full obedience, he therefore allows his compromises to bear their bitter fruit. Just as earlier God intervened in Lot's life when he was quite happy living comfortably in his compromised situation in Sodom, so also Jacob found himself suffering the consequences of his compromises.

THE BENEFIT OF SUFFERED CONSEQUENCES

Isn't that sometimes true of ourselves also? Satan tells you that you can compromise and get away with it. "You'll never get caught!" he whispers. "If you do, you won't suffer the consequences of your actions. No one will care." But Satan is a liar. Sin does have consequences. Very often those consequences are awful. If we listen to Satan's counsel and give in to sin, then frequently we will suffer them. Why? The reason is because God loves you too much to let you get away with sin. That would confirm you in your compromise. Instead, God disciplines us as a loving father, to wean us from our addiction to sin. Sometimes, therefore, he allows us to experience the weight of our sinfulness so that we may turn away from it.

But even though bearing some of the consequences of our sin may have a positive, sobering effect on us, what awful, ugly things those consequences of sin often are! These consequences may not involve only us but also our children. I've seen Christian men who have destroyed their families through adultery and divorce and daily live with the pain of the consequences of their actions, not just in their lives but in the lives of their children. In Jacob's case, before it was all said and done, the bitter fruits of his sin involved rape, pillage, and murder. All of this sequence was because he stopped twenty miles short of full obedience. His personal failure led to disastrous consequences for the whole family.

THE RAPE OF DINAH

It all started with Dinah. She went out to see the women of the land (Gen. 34:1). The Hebrew suggests that this was a single incident, not a regular occurrence. She was perhaps curious to check out what the local social scene was like. But this seemingly innocent act of curiosity ended in disaster. Instead of seeing the women of the land, she was seen by one of the men of the land, Shechem, who was the son of the ruler of the city (Gen. 34:2). Just as in the first sin (Gen. 3:6), seeing quickly led to taking the desired but forbidden fruit. Shechem took Dinah and lay with her and violated her, a sequence of three verbs whose rapid succession mirrors the events they describe. The act of passion was over almost as soon as it began.

However, unlike the case of Amnon and Tamar in 2 Samuel 13, where long-simmering lust led to rape and then sudden revulsion and hatred, in this case the sudden lust was transformed into the more enduring positive emotion of love. Shechem became emotionally attached to the girl and spoke kindly to her (Gen. 34:3). Shechem was not merely after her body as a sexual object; he wanted to marry her, and he asked his father to seek her hand on his behalf.

Shechem's proposal may seem nothing short of bizarre to us, with our modern Western views of courtship and marriage. What self-respecting woman would be willing to undertake a relationship under those circumstances, we may think? However, the parallel with Amnon and Tamar is helpful here too, as this outcome is what she requested Amnon to do for her. Marriage, even a marriage contracted under such an initial cloud, was better than the alternative of being perpetually viewed as damaged goods and therefore probably being left forever in the socially perilous position of being an aging single woman. Shechem's proposal at least showed that he wanted to make reparation for his act of passion and, to use the old-fashioned phrase, to make an honest woman out of Dinah.

HAMOR'S PROPOSAL

Jacob heard of Dinah's defilement but failed to act immediately and decisively in response to the news; instead, he hesitated and waited until his sons returned from the fields. One wonders if he would have responded differently if Dinah had been Rachel's daughter and not Leah's. His lack of reaction contrasted strongly to the reaction of his sons, who were filled with fury. Such a thing was disgraceful and ought not to have been done in (or against) Israel, they said (Gen. 34:7). Indeed, it ought not. But disgraceful things happen regularly in a fallen world, especially if you choose to settle down next to a pagan city (Gen. 33:18). It was no use at this point yelling over spilled milk.

In the light of Shechem's proposal for Dinah's hand in marriage, the important question that faced them now was What do we do next? For what Hamor, the father of Shechem, was putting on the table for negotiation was far more than a single marriage proposal: it was the offer of becoming a single community. The Israelites and the Shechemites would live together as one people, intermarrying with one another and sharing a common destiny. The phrase that in Genesis 13:9 was the precursor to the division of two families, "Is not the whole land before you?" here became the potential precursor to the union of two families (Gen. 34:10). What Hamor offered Israel was an apparent shortcut to possessing the land through intermarriage. Significantly, the verb he used in Genesis 34:10, *achaz* ("acquire property"), is related to the word for "possession" in God's promise of the land to Abraham as an eternal inheritance in Genesis 17:8 (*achuzzah*).

Efforts were even made to make sure that Shechem's sin against Dinah and her people should not be an obstacle to the negotiations. Shechem came forward and humbly asked that he might find favor in the eyes of Jacob and his sons and make appropriate restitution for his offense (Gen. 34:11–12). The fact that such forgiveness and favor was what Jacob sought and received from Esau (Gen. 33:10) would have given added weight to his words.

But when the offer is seen in the light of the bigger picture, it is clear that Jacob and his sons could not accept what Hamor was offering. The land was not to be received through intermarriage with the inhabitants of the land but through God's gift. Shechem's sin could perhaps have been forgiven and friendly relationships could have been restored, just as they had been with Esau, but Jacob's family could no more join into a single people with Shechem than they had with Esau. Their calling was to be a distinct community from those who dwelled in the land. They should therefore have declined Shechem's advances courteously, explaining the reasons for their decision clearly.

In the process, the opportunity for them to be a blessing to the nations around them might have been real. They could have told Hamor and Shechem of their God and his promise and how crucial that promise was to their self-identity as a people. They could perhaps even have invited Shechem to become a worshiper of their God and to be incorporated into his people by faith. Although God's people were not to intermarry with pagans, the door was always open to pagans to leave their prior allegiances and become part of God's people, as the examples of Rahab and Ruth later demonstrated. This could have been an awesome opportunity for Jacob to share from his experience the good news of the grace of their God and the forgiveness he offers to sinners who come to him in repentance and faith.

A DECEITFUL STRATEGY

Instead of responding with gracious truth, however, Jacob's sons responded with a disgraceful strategy. They had learned well at their father's knee. The children inherit the sins of the parents, often in greater measure. From Adam's sin in eating the fruit, we move quickly on to murder in the next generation with Cain and the glorification of gratuitous violence in song by the seventh generation with Lamech (Gen. 4:23–24). Just as Jacob deceived his father in order to steal his brother's birthright (Gen. 27:35), so now Jacob's sons deceived Hamor in order to massacre the unsuspecting citizens of Shechem (Gen. 34:14). Given this trajectory of sin, Joseph was later extremely fortunate that his brothers only sold him into slavery. They were capable of much worse. We sow the wind; our children reap the whirlwind. What sins are your children inheriting in magnified form from you?

What is more, the deceitful response of Jacob's sons was cloaked in the form of religion, and the true religion at that. Jacob maintained his religious practices while stopping short of full obedience, and his sons went further, using their religion to help them destroy their enemies. What violence and sin has been and is carried on in religion's name! Wars have been fought and massacres committed in the name of Christianity, as well as other faiths. So it is here also. Jacob's sons started out with a true statement and an appropriate response to Hamor's proposal: "We can't do such a thing; we can't give our sister to a man who is uncircumcised. That would be a disgrace to us" (Gen. 34:14). That much was true. Marriage outside the covenant community would not have been appropriate. But instead of requiring an internal change in Hamor as a prerequisite for marriage, they asked for an external change. All they asked for was that the sign of the covenant should be applied to every male of the community through circumcision.

Motivated by his delight in Dinah, Shechem responded with alacrity. He and his father went to the city gate, where the important people would gather to make decisions, and put the proposal of Jacob's sons to the men of the city (Gen. 34:19–23). They sold the deal to their fellow citizens on the basis of the financial benefits of incorporating this new group, and ironically also on the supposed peaceable disposition of the Israelites (Gen. 34:21). It was made clear to all concerned that there were no religious implications involved in the act of circumcision; it was viewed as a weird cultural hang-up the Israelites had, a mere formality (Gen. 34:22). After this formality was out of the way, then the two peoples would become one.

Neither side took the preciousness of the covenant sign of circumcision seriously. Such an attitude may be what we would expect from pagans, but what a sad commentary this is on the spiritual state of Jacob and his family. Up until now, they had apparently made no efforts to share their faith with the Shechemites so that they might appropriately be circumcised and become part of the covenant community. Now they used the religious form of circumcision to give themselves an unfair advantage, so that Simeon and Levi could more easily massacre the unsuspecting inhabitants of Shechem. Circumcision was supposed to be a mark of their covenant separation from the nations; here, however, they offered to become one nation with the Canaanites, not on condition that the Canaanites shared their faith but on condition that the Canaanites shared their religious practices.

Is that not also a danger in the contemporary church? Sometimes we are so eager to bring the seekers into the church that we reduce the requirements of entry to the lowest common denominator. For fear of offending people, we may open the Lord's table to any who wish to partake, whether or not they have publicly committed themselves to Christ and his church, or we may even baptize the children of any who come to us, whether or not the parents have a credible profession of faith. However, if we do that, we may end up obliterating the line that separates us from those outside the covenant community and therefore all need for the seekers to move further on to become disciples. Discipleship is sometimes presented as if it were an optional extra for a few Type A Christians, instead of being an essential mark of all those who are Christians. In the process, we may end up building a bigger religious program but may fail to fulfill the commission that we have received as Christ's church.

Though Simeon's and Levi's brothers were not involved in the massacre, they were happy enough to join in plundering the city, carrying off everything that wasn't nailed down (Gen. 34:27–29). Selective morality is everywhere evident. They were outraged at the defilement Shechem had imposed on Dinah but not apparently at the defilement they inflicted on themselves by stripping the corpses (Gen. 34:27). Flocks, herds, donkeys, wealth: everything that was in the city was fair game, including the women and children (Gen. 34:29). The initial sin of taking one woman was returned in kind but in multiplied form. It is clear that the Israelites were not in any way morally better than the present inhabitants of the Promised Land.

JACOB'S RESPONSE

How did Jacob respond to this outrageous behavior on the part of his sons, as head of the family? Not a word of moral outrage passed his lips. In fact, Jacob is passive and silent almost throughout the chapter. Finally he broke his silence with this gem of a moral pronouncement:

> You have brought trouble on me by making me a stench to the Canaanites and Perizzites, the people living in this land. We are few in number, and if they join forces against me and attack me, I and my household will be destroyed. (Gen. 34:30)

Did you notice the pronouns in his speech? They are almost all "I" or "me" (even more so in Hebrew, where the "we" is literally "I"). It was not their sin that he hated and deplored. Rather, it was the possible negative effects that their crime might have on him. He viewed what they had done as a tactical blunder rather than as a sin against a holy God. In fact, the brothers raised the question of morality in their response to Jacob: "Should he have treated our sister like a prostitute?" (Gen. 34:31). And Jacob was once again silent. He seems to accept their lame self-justification, which exaggerated the scope of Shechem's original offense and ignored all of his efforts at reconciliation and restitution. Is the sin of one man, for which he attempted to atone and make restitution, a sufficient reason for the extermination of a community? Who appointed them as agents of divine judgment? Where would Jacob and his family have been if Esau had reacted similarly to Jacob's efforts to restore their damaged relationship?

Up and down. Success and failure. What are we to make of Jacob? One minute he is Israel, striving with God and man and overcoming. The next minute, he is a compromising and compromised bystander to an atrocity. What are we to say except that he looks a lot like us? Maybe our downs aren't as deep as his. Perhaps we haven't personally presided over such a massacre. But then maybe our ups aren't as high either. We are altogether more mediocre saints and mediocre sinners. You could blame his environment, growing up in a home where favoritism and deceit was rife. Or you can blame his heredity, which stretches back to Adam and Eve, the first sinners. There is plenty of blame to go around. Either way, however, the good news is that God hasn't finished with Jacob yet.

Isn't that an amazing fact? In spite of his continuing sinfulness, the deceived deceiver is not abandoned by *El elohe yisrael*, the mighty God of Israel. In spite of his continuing failure, he is not stamped "rejected" and placed on the shelf. On the contrary, God again appears to him (Gen. 35:1) and takes him limping back to the beginning, back to Bethel, back to the place where it all began. There Jacob will be reminded of his weakness, the thread by which his life once hung, when he was fleeing for his life from his brother with nothing other than the clothes he stood up in. There he will be called upon to build the altar he had vowed to build and offer up on it a sacrifice.

SHECHEM AND THE SOLUTION FOR SIN

How do you deal with the problem of sin? The narrative ends with a question that is left unresolved and hanging. Neither Jacob nor his sons have an adequate solution to deal with sin. One way is to massacre the sinner, as Dinah's brothers did. Let the whole people die for the sins of its prince. This is one natural human response to the offensiveness of sin, and there is a certain justice to it. This is the approach to moral disorder that is normally favored by political conservatives: let's get tough on crime. The problem is that it doesn't establish a lasting peace, however. It doesn't deal with sin in any profound sense; it only obliterates the sinner. However, if Jacob's sons are the moral hardliners on this issue, Jacob is merely pragmatically soft. He would rather avoid dealing with sin because of the messy effects such action may have in his life. This is the approach normally favored by political liberals. Let the sinner go untouched, is their solution. "After all," they would say, "we have to understand the difficult background from which he comes. His parents were Canaanites, after all. What do you expect from someone brought up under these circumstances?"

Neither the way of pragmatic softness nor the way of moral hardness solves the problem of sin, however. One way destroys the sinner; the other way treats too lightly the sin. In this case, the result of the brothers' rough justice is the destruction of the sinner not his salvation, the mocking of God's name not its glorification. The one who defiled Israel is destroyed, but no one is purified. Nor would Jacob's way have been any better.

Is there another way to deal with sin? Is there a way that treats the awfulness of sin with appropriate seriousness yet still reaches out and redeems the sinner? Indeed there is! God's way is for a substitutionary sacrifice to be made. A sinless sacrifice, one without spot or blemish, must be put to death in the place of the sinner. For Jacob, when he finally stood before the altar at Bethel, the substitute was a lamb. The spotless lamb took his place and was offered up for his sins. As Jacob offered it up there, must he not have cast his mind back to the stories his father, Isaac, had told him, of the day on another mountain when Isaac was almost offered up? Then too God provided a lamb in his place. The wages of sin are death, and they must be paid; sin is serious business. But they do not have to be paid by us; provided there is a spotless substitute to take our place, the sinner can be redeemed.

So also for us, God has provided a lamb. Jesus Christ, the Lamb of God without spot or blemish, was offered up for us on the cross. Instead of the people dying for the sins of their prince, as happened at Shechem, the King of kings has died for the sins of his people. That is God's way of dealing with sin once and for all, yet at the same time still saving the sinners. It is a method so complete that it can deal even with the sin of compromised and compromising Jacob and his family. It is a method so complete that it can deal with your sin and my sin too, no matter what you may have done. No one is beyond reach of this redemption. The God of Bethel is mighty to forgive all of our sins and receive us into his presence, through the death of the Lamb of God, Jesus Christ.

FOR FURTHER REFLECTION

1. Why is it sometimes a good thing to suffer the consequences of our sin?
2. Why couldn't Jacob and Shechem "just get along"? What are some of the limits on our involvement with the world?

3. How might we be tempted to use religion as a cloak to promote our interests?
4. In what ways do we fail to deal properly with sin within the covenant community?
5. What is God's answer to such gross sin?

II

BACK TO BASICS

(GENESIS 35)

In the mid-1990s, the then British Prime Minister, John Major, issued a stirring call to the nation to return to traditional moral values. He titled his call "Back to Basics." It was a call that came back to haunt him as a succession of members of his government were caught in embarrassing moral lapses, until the question was asked whether John Major really understood what "Back to Basics" meant. There is no doubt, however, what "Back to Basics" meant for Jacob. It was a call for him and his family to return to their spiritual roots, to go back to Bethel and be reconciled to God. Jacob had been drifting for far too long. It was ten or fifteen years since he had returned to the Promised Land and been restored to a good relationship with Esau. Yet he had put off and put off going on to Bethel and fulfilling his vow to God. As so often happens, it took a crisis in his life to bring him back to God.

THROUGH HARDSHIP TO OBEDIENCE

Why is it so often that way? Why does God have to lead us through such hard roads to bring us to obedience? Is it perhaps because we too are a stubborn and stiff-necked people, like Israel and his children? It just might be! In Jacob's life, the crisis that turned him around was Dinah's rape by Shechem and the subsequent slaughter of the Shechemites by his sons. Humanly speaking, that could have been the end of the story for Israel. They were heavily outnumbered by the surrounding inhabitants of the land. If the Canaanites and Perizzites had come seeking vengeance, then the whole family could easily have been massacred. But there was no attempt to exact reprisals. Why not? It was because of God's protection of Jacob and his family (Gen. 35:5). God caused a holy fear of them to fall on the surrounding nations, just as he had earlier intervened to keep Jacob safe from the wrath of Laban. Jacob's worries for his safety (Gen. 34:30) were unnecessary, because he had failed to take God into account.

What this crisis did was to stir up Jacob into an act of decisive spiritual leadership, of a kind that was absent in Genesis 34. It was not the crisis by itself that brought about the change in Jacob, though. Many people go through horrendous experiences without being transformed by them. What changed Jacob was the gracious initiative of God, who came once again seeking the lost sinner. Do you see how amazing the first words of Genesis 35 are? "Then God said to Jacob . . ." Jacob had blown it again; he had first allowed the commercial attractions of Shechem to prevent him from doing his spiritual duty at Bethel, and then he had abdicated proper leadership in his family, allowing his sons to run amok. But in the midst of that personal and family chaos, God graciously spoke to him, calling him back to his relationship with himself.

Isn't that how real change always happens? The first step in spiritual renewal, as in spiritual birth, always comes from God. Left to ourselves, our hearts are cold as ice toward God. We rapidly slide into compromise and embrace the attractions of false goals and idols. The second law of thermodynamics, which declares that matter always proceeds from order into disorder, applies to our souls as much as to the rest of our world. But God . . . our God will not abandon those whom he has chosen, those with whom he has made a covenant. So he comes to us, just as he came to Jacob, and calls us back to him, to renew our walk with him.

What is more, our God is endlessly patient with his people. This is not the first time that God has intervened in Jacob's life in this way. A similar pattern was at work at the end of Genesis 30. There too Jacob had settled comfortably into material success in the employ of Laban, apparently completely forgetting about God's promises and the Promised Land (Gen. 30:43). At that time too, God brought a crisis into his life, which caused his comfortable sloth to be disturbed, and after that came and graciously called him to renewed faithfulness to his commitments (Gen. 31:3). Is there a similar pattern in your life? I know that there is in mine. We repeatedly slip away from passionately pursuing God into the pursuit of other things and are enveloped by a comfortable lukewarmness, until God intervenes through trials and failed temptations and calls us back to himself.

THE CALL TO PURITY

Jacob heard the call of God and extended it to his household. Get up, get rid of all your foreign gods, purify yourselves, and come, let us go up and worship! After the repeated theme of defilement in the previous chapter, now the time has come to focus on purification. The same call to purity that Jacob issued to his family is extended to each of us in Psalm 24:3–6:

Who may ascend the hill of the LORD?
Who may stand in his holy place?

> He who has clean hands and a pure heart,
>> who does not lift up his soul to an idol
>> or swear by what is false.
> He will receive blessing from the LORD
>> and vindication from God his Savior.
> Such is the generation of those who seek him,
>> who seek your face, O God of Jacob.

The connections between this passage and the Jacob narrative go far beyond the mention of the "God of Jacob." The psalm talks of someone who does not swear "deceitfully" (NASB—*mirmah;* v. 4), a key word in Jacob's story (see Gen. 27:35; 29:25; 34:13). Such a person is able to stand in God's holy place (*maqom*), just as Jacob did at Bethel (Gen. 28:11), and seeks God's face, thereby desiring to replicate Jacob's encounter with God at Peniel (Gen. 32:30). He will receive God's blessing, the goal of all of Jacob's striving.

The person who is accepted by God is thus in some ways like Jacob; more precisely, he is like the Israel that Jacob is being transformed into by grace, literally receiving righteousness (*tsedaqah,* which the NIV translates "vindication") from God his Savior. This righteousness is not something that is intrinsically his own; it is the gift of God. Yet as with Jacob in Genesis 35, the call of God necessarily flows out in the believer into a life of renewed purification. Changed hearts necessarily lead to changed behavior. As those who have received God's grace, you and I are called to put aside the things that are polluting us and destroying us and to go back to basics. We are called daily to renew our first love, to lay to rest the other things that so easily distract us and pursue a face-to-face encounter with God, so that by his grace we may receive his blessing.

Purification begins with burying your idols, all those souvenirs of our former ways of living and thinking that we have brought along on the journey, just like Rachel (see Gen. 31:19). There is a reason why the Ten Commandments begin with insistent claims: "I am the LORD your God who brought you out of Egypt, out of the land of slavery. You shall have no other gods before me. You shall not make for yourself an idol in the form of anything in heaven above or on the earth beneath or in the waters below" (Exod. 20:2–4). A pure heart begins with true worship of the living God and cannot be separated from it. This is the mistake John Major made, a common mistake in our culture, when he assumed that people could be called to adopt a basic morality without the foundation of the gospel. The result of such an appeal is, at best, a legalism that is powerless to effect deep changes in people's lives. It may perhaps hide sin, but it cannot deal with sin. The law alone, even if it is God's perfect law, cannot sanctify. On the contrary, it often tends to provoke lawbreaking (Rom. 7:7–12). True purity of heart flows out of the life-changing power of the gospel. We are set free to serve as we recognize more fully the true nature of the God whom we serve and bury the old idolatries that have tied us down.

This freedom to serve is symbolized in the case of Jacob and his family by the act of changing clothing (Gen. 35:2). This symbolic act of changing clothing becomes the basis for Paul's metaphor of the changed life in Ephesians, a life that consists of putting off the old self, corrupted as it is with deceitful desires, and putting on the new self, created to be like God in true righteousness and holiness (Eph. 4:24). This happens, Paul tells us, not through moral exertion alone but through renewed thinking (Eph. 4:23). Paul's point is that the Christian life is far more than obedience to a set of don'ts. A life of don'ts puts off the old and leaves us naked! The Christian life is to be marked by dos as well as don'ts, by a beautiful array of Christian virtues, the fruits of the Spirit, as well as a passionate fleeing from the vices with which this world surrounds us. It is to be motivated by minds and hearts that have been transformed by an encounter with the living God. His love is what drives us now, not the old idolatries of our hearts.

THE AMAZING GRACE OF BETHEL

The truly amazing aspect of this call to renewed purity is that Bethel is still accessible to sinful compromisers like Jacob and like us. Our sinful hearts are such that even when we bury our idols, we never forget where we buried them and tend to go back regularly to lay flowers on their grave! Yet there is abundant grace available for you and me. Even though we neglect him and fall away, still God remains faithful to his covenant promises and calls you back to him. Indeed, that is a basic biblical principle: God remains faithful to his Word, even when we are unfaithful. In the midst of the total destruction of the city of Jerusalem that resulted in 586 B.C. from a long history of unfaithfulness on the part of God's people, the author of Lamentations took heart from this truth. He said, "Because of the LORD's great love we are not consumed, for his compassions never fail. They are new every morning; great is your faithfulness" (Lam. 3:22–23).

That is Jacob's testimony to his family: Because of the Lord's great love we are not consumed; great is his faithfulness. So now we're going up to Bethel to build an altar to the God who answered me in the day of my distress and who has been with me wherever I have gone (Gen. 35:3). God had been faithful to Jacob. God appeared to him first at Bethel, when he was on the run from Esau, when it seemed that all was lost. God had been with him throughout his life's journey, just as he had promised, in spite of Jacob's continual compromising and half-hearted obedience. Now God had fulfilled the promise made to him at Bethel and brought him back there, not as he left it, with nothing but the clothes he stood up in, but now with a family of twelve sons and much wealth. God had indeed been faithful to his promise, and Jacob's response was to worship.

While he was worshiping, God appeared to Jacob once more at Bethel and renewed his covenant with him (Gen. 35:9–13). God met with him there and reminded him of the transforming new name he had been given at Peniel. It is as if he said, "Other people may name you Jacob, but as for me, I have named you Israel." God's good work in his life, once begun, could not be halted. There God pronounced his blessing upon Jacob in the same words that his father, Isaac, had used in his blessing so many years before: "Be fruitful and increase in number" (Gen. 35:11; see 28:3). But now a new element is added: "Kings will come from your body" (Gen. 35:11). God's grace is overwhelming in its kindness. In place of Jacob's ill-fated efforts to buy a piece of the Promised Land for himself at Shechem (Gen. 33:19), God announced that he would give it to him and to his descendants.

God's transforming work of blessing would even extend to Jacob's family. Though his family had thus far been a model of discord and infighting, God announced that from him would come a community of nations, again as Isaac had asked in Genesis 28:3. As we saw in Genesis 28, it is not too strong to translate this phrase as a "church of nations": a covenant community of God's people, bound together in a spiritual unity. We may say that the blessings that are promised to all nations through the original blessing on Abraham (Gen. 12:2–3) come to his spiritual heirs as they are incorporated into the new community of the children of Israel, the church.

UNPROMISING BEGINNINGS

What an unpromising beginning this must have seemed, though, for such a big plan! Like Sarah before him, must Jacob not have been tempted to laugh secretly at the audacity of God's Word (see Gen. 18:12)? If we did not know the end of the story, would we be inclined to believe it? Can a spiritual community bonded together in peace and harmony really come from Jacob's family? What a joke! Wouldn't that be an even more impossible dream than that a ninety-year-old should bear a son? Yet we serve a God who persistently uses such unpromising beginnings to bring about his wonderful ends, so that it may be seen clearly that all is of him.

This is a principle that gives us hope whenever we face unpromising beginnings, difficult middles, and dark futures in our personal or church experience. The normal zip code of the church in this present age is not the idealistic but imaginary utopia we so often read about in Christian books and magazines. Rather, it is the real world of wreckage and ruins and chaos. Our personal lives are full of half-hidden brokenness. The church as we know it is made up of damaged people who together form deeply flawed institutions. We are all too often far more Jacob's children than the Israel of God.

For those of us involved in pastoral ministry, first discovering this reality is frequently an enormous shock, one more thing they never told us in seminary. Yet it remains also true that out of and among those ruins, God is nonetheless at work in the lives of his people. The Scottish preacher J. S. Stewart gives us a powerful illustration of this truth:

> In one of George MacDonald's books, there is a woman who has met a sudden sorrow. "I wish I'd never been made!" she exclaims petulantly and bitterly: to which her friend quietly replies, "My dear, you're not made yet. You're only being made—and this is the Maker's process."[1]

---

1 George MacDonald, *The Strong Name* (London: Hodder and Stoughton, 1941), 145.

We are not made yet, we're only being made—and the Maker's process is to take us through trials and temptations, sorrows and setbacks. As we are shown our brokenness and emptiness more fully, we come to cling more tightly still to God's promise that one day the work in us and in our world will be perfectly done. Though his people are deeply divided in the present, God's purpose and promise still stand, reiterated in the New Testament, to make all of us one in Christ Jesus. Though now our churches are still all too often the new Jacob and very much works in progress, yet in Christ the new name Israel will ultimately describe us accurately. Christ will build his church, and the gates of hell will not prevail against it (Matt. 16:18). We cannot and must not despair of ourselves or of others when we serve such an awesome God!

It is this self-revelation of God in all his graciousness that moved Jacob again to worship. How could it not? How can you experience God's grace and *not* be forced to your knees in adoration? How can you see again the depths of your sin, and see the Savior's nail-pierced hand stretched out to pick you up out of the muck, and not be touched at the core of your being? So once again, as he had so many years before, Jacob raised a stone pillar to mark the place where God had met with him and poured out offerings of oil and wine upon it. He had finally come home to worship at God's house. He was back in Bethel.

LIFE AFTER REPENTANCE

Jacob had repented of his sins and returned to God. He was back in the center of obedience to God's Word again. However, that did not mean that he was thereby exempt from the pains and sorrows of life. Even full obedience does not guarantee comfort and an easy life. As Jacob arrived at the holy place, he buried his mother's faithful nurse, Deborah (Gen. 35:8). As he left it, he buried his beloved wife, Rachel (Gen. 35:19). The journey to and from the house of God, Bethel, was thus bracketed by two gravestones. Death, the result of the curse on Adam and Eve's sin, is our constant companion in Genesis.

Rachel died in childbirth, giving birth to her second son. Her earlier words to Jacob, "Give me sons, or I'll die" (Gen. 30:1), could stand as a fitting epitaph for her. With her last words she named her son Ben-oni, "son of my affliction." Jacob, however, renamed him Benjamin, "son of my right hand"—a much more positive evaluation (Gen. 35:18). Jacob knew for himself the power of a name and longed for a good future for his last son. With that, Jacob's family is complete; he now has twelve sons.

Jacob's life was still not free from conflict, however. His eldest son, Reuben, disgraced himself and the family by sleeping with his father's concubine Bilhah (Gen. 35:22). This was probably not a moment of passion but rather a political act, an attempt by the eldest son to usurp his father's role and take over the leadership position. Absalom did the same thing in 2 Samuel 16:21–22. Once again we are clearly being shown in the earliest recorded acts of Jacob's children that God's purposes for them will not be earned through their wonderful merits but bestowed as a gift of God's grace.

With Jacob's return to Bethel and to full obedience, the spotlight naturally moves on to the next generation. Will they learn the same lessons their father learned? Will they be committed to his God? At this point, it is still an open question. Israel's obedience is never more secure than the obedience of the current generation. There is never any room for complacency; when one generation has been reached, it is time to move on to the next. So it is also in the church. We can never be content saying, "As for me, I will serve the Lord." It is not even enough for us to be able to say, "As for me and my spouse, we will serve the Lord." Like Joshua, we need to have a passion for spiritual things that is transmitted to everyone with whom we have contact, but especially to our children, so that we too can say, "As for me and my household, we will serve the LORD" (Josh. 24:15).

Finally Jacob came home to his father, Isaac, at Mamre and lived with him for the remainder of Isaac's life (Gen. 35:27). When Isaac died, Jacob and Esau buried him. That generation had been reconciled.

It is interesting to note that Esau does not become irrelevant to the biblical writer after he has ceased to be a threat to Jacob. His future too is worth recording. The concern to record the lasting reconciliation of Jacob and Esau, along with the lengthy and detailed genealogy of Esau's family in Genesis 36, implies that even while the line of Esau is outside of the promise, it is not outside the reach of God's mercy. If all nations will be blessed through Abraham, may that blessing not begin within Abraham's wider family, including Esau and his descendants? Israel was later explicitly commanded not to look down on Esau's descendants, the Edomites (Deut. 23:7). Even though there are great and precious promises to the children of the faith community, God's concern is never limited to those born into that privileged position. Outsiders too may receive God's mercy and grace and be added to the family of God.

THE CHANGING OF THE GUARD

In many ways, Jacob's key role in God's plan was at an end. With Isaac's death, we end the history of the patriarchal period and come to the beginning of the history of Israel proper. The appearance of God to Jacob at Bethel marks the end of the revelation to the patriarchs. God will not directly reveal himself to man again until he meets with Moses at the burning bush (Exod. 3). That doesn't mean that God is not active, however. Far from it! He intervenes and overrules repeatedly in the life of Joseph to secure the long-term future of his people. He continues to direct events through dreams and interpretations and various other forms of providence. But there is no more face-to-face contact between God and his people. They now have to live on the strength of the promises once delivered to the saints.

What kind of future may we expect for Israel's children, based on the hints we have already seen? They have not made an auspicious start. First it was Simeon and Levi putting an unsuspecting city to the sword. Then we found Reuben sleeping with his father's concubine. Whatever will they think of next? Well, how about selling their least favorite brother as a slave, and Judah sleeping with his daughter-in-law, having mistaken her for a prostitute? They are not a promising group, are they? What nation ever had a less positive impression of its ancestors than Israel? They are in truth Jacob's children. But that's the point, isn't it? God can take people like these and use them to do his will, and ultimately to create his church. As Joseph put it in Genesis 50:20: "You intended to harm me, but God intended it for good." God's sovereign purpose prevails even in the lives of wicked people.

This is the wonderful truth of relentless grace. God's plan does not depend on him finding suitably willing and holy implements to employ. He is able to accomplish his purposes even with the most deeply flawed individuals. Even sinners cannot stand in his way and frustrate him. Where is that more vividly seen than on the cross? There, though Satan did his worst, though God's people and the Gentiles allied themselves against him, all they were able to do was what God had planned all along. God's work of redemption was accomplished! Christ's perfect life was offered up as an acceptable sacrifice to God the Father in our place. By that act, we are saved. Jacob and all of his spiritual children are redeemed by sovereign, relentless grace.

What a comfort there is in God's relentless grace! Are you discouraged by the problems you see all around you? Are you downcast by the sin that you see in your heart? Go back to Bethel with Jacob and bow down before the God who remains committed to you, in spite of your many faults. Go back to the cross and bow down before the God who took upon himself your sins and nailed them to the tree once and for all. Then look up and behold the greatness of the salvation that awaits you and me. We shall be clothed in spotless robes of Christ's righteousness, made fit to stand in God's presence forever—and no one and nothing in heaven or on earth can stand in the way of God's declared purpose to make it so. If God is thus for us, who can stand against us? How awesome it is to know that everything rests in the hands of God Almighty and that through us, with all of our sins and failures, he will still accomplish his perfect purposes for our salvation and for his glory!

FOR FURTHER REFLECTION

1. How has God intervened in your life to call you back to fellowship and obedience?
2. What is the only foundation for real life change? Why?
3. What difference does it make for you to know that the normal location of the church is not Utopia but the real world of wreckage and ruins?
4. Overall, how does the story of Jacob point us again and again to God's relentless grace? Why is that important?
5. What are the main lessons you have learned from this study?

INDEX OF SCRIPTURE